Published in 2014 by Voyageur Press, an imprint of Quarto Publishing Group USA Inc.,
400 First Avenue North, Suite 400, Minneapolis, MN 55401 USA

Voyageur Press titles are also available at discounts in bulk quantity for industrial or
sales-promotional use. For details write to Special Sales Manager at Quarto Publishing
Group USA Inc., 400 First Avenue North, Suite 400, Minneapolis, MN 55401 USA.

To find out more about our books, visit us online at www.voyageurpress.com.

ISBN-13: 978-0-7603-4578-8

Library of Congress Cataloging-in-Publication Data

Comfort food cookbook / edited by Karen K. Will, Grit magazine.
     pages cm
 Recipes from the archives of Grit magazine.
 ISBN 978-0-7603-4578-8 (softcover)
 1. Cooking, American. 2. Comfort food. I. Will, Karen K., editor of compilation. II. Grit (Topeka, Kan.)
 TX715.C3173 2014
 641.5973--dc23
                              2013048352

Front cover photo: Pot Roast: *Karen Will*; Amish Acres Bean Soup: *Nitr/Fotolia*;
Rhubarb Streusel Pie: *istockphoto.com/Innershadows*
Back cover photos: Applesauce Doughnuts: *Karen Will*; Southern Fried Chicken: *Monkey Business/ Fotolia*; Old-Fashioned Green Beans: *iStockphoto.com/HittProductions*; Soft Pretzels: *Karen Will*

Editors: Karen K. Will, Elizabeth Noll
Design Manager: James Kegley
Cover: Gavin Duffy
Design: Carol Holtz
Layout: Kazuko Collins

Printed in China

10 9 8 7 6 5 4 3 2 1

COMFORT FOOD
COOKBOOK

230 Recipes for Bringing Classic Good Food to the Table

Edited by Karen K. Will, GRIT Magazine

Voyageur
Press

Contents

Preface

Where I grew up, on the border between New Mexico and what we called "Old Mexico," food was an adventure. To say our traditional dishes were spicy is like saying a cholla cactus is prickly. The word is far too mild to describe the trauma.

As a kid growing up in this aggressive culinary environment, I learned that my refuge was the tortilla. When I got a bite that was too hot, water was of no use. Capsaicin—the substance that makes chiles hot—is a waxy compound, which repels water and water-based liquids and makes them worthless for cooling one's tongue. A big gulp of milk helped a little. But the surest cure for a burning tongue was a warm, soft tortilla infused with lard.

My grandparents' best friends were Roman and Eva Mendez. They lived about half a mile from us, over one sand hill in our tiny village of Anapra, New Mexico. We visited them once a week or so, and usually sat around for an hour or two, in the manner of that time, eating, drinking, and enjoying each other's company.

I tagged along for the tortillas. Eva Mendez had a way with tortillas. Eva's tortillas were a revelation, a monument, a tribute to everything that alkaline water and white flour can become.

A lot of families already were using canned shortening, but not Eva. Her tortillas were made with lard, and they were delicious. I didn't want butter on them. I didn't want honey. The unleavened white bread, warm from the skillet, was more tantalizing than any cookie, candy, or cake—and the perfect medicine for a tender mouth that has recently come in contact with a chunk of jalapeno.

For me it's the essence of comfort food: Comforting in more ways than one.

Bryan Welch
Publisher of *Grit* magazine
Topeka, Kansas

Acknowledgments

Following the success of our first book, *Lard: The Lost Art of Cooking with Your Grandmother's Secret Ingredient*, the *Grit* and *Capper's Farmer* team was eager to keep the momentum going. *Comfort Food Cookbook* was the result.

This cookbook is a tribute to the thousands of readers who've contributed recipes to our magazines. Without their creative passion and generosity over a span of more than 130 years—up to and including this year—this cookbook would not have been possible.

Many thanks to our publisher, Bryan Welch; to our editorial team, including senior associate editor Traci Smith, associate editor Jean Teller, and generations of other food editors, and most especially our lead project editor, Karen Will, for sifting through thousands of recipes; to our social media experts, including former *Grit* web editor Natalie Gould, current *Grit* web editor Kellsey Trimble, and *Capper's Farmer* web editor Sarah Sinning; to *Grit* and *Capper's Farmer* managing editor Caleb Regan; and to our editorial assistant, Ilene Reid.

Thanks are also due to Andrew Perkins, who managed the compilation and editing process, and to Brandy Ernzen for her public relations work.

We are grateful that Voyageur Press was willing to take a chance on this project. Thanks for turning *Comfort Food Cookbook* into the gem it is.

And finally, thanks to you, dear reader. Without you, this book would have no meaning.

Hank Will
Editor-in-chief, *Grit* and *Capper's Farmer* magazines.

Introduction

There was a time when comfort food didn't exist. I don't mean to say that folks didn't enjoy certain dishes or that certain dishes didn't elicit happy, warm feelings. I mean that once upon a time food was food. Good food was really good, and in many cases it was also comforting—both physically and psychologically. I'm quite sure that the stacks and stacks of flapjacks Royal and Almanzo Wilder consumed in Laura Ingalls Wilder's *The Long Winter* were indeed a form of comfort food. My goodness, those boys could pack them away. Good thing they could, because they needed all the energy they could get to survive those many subzero days and nights.

There is no doubt that Almanzo Wilder enjoyed what we call comfort food while he was growing up, too. In *Farmer Boy*, many of Almanzo's daily childhood adventures are punctuated with fantastic farm-table fare. Certain items, such as pies of various types and roasted meat, so captivated the hard-working and growing boy that he would sometimes daydream about them while working all morning, anticipating the noontime dinner bell. Obviously Almanzo needed the calories, but he also craved some foods because they comforted him psychologically. There was nothing like coming in from evening chores to a supper sandwich topped off with Mom's warm apple pie.

But I don't think the Wilder boys thought about food the way we do today, in twenty-first-century categories. In modern times, some characterize comfort food as food that's high in sugar—that gives a sugar rush, if you will, eliciting a comforting response and stoking our desire for it. Others say comfort foods are the high-carbohydrate dishes that we crave when things look a little gray outside and blue inside our own heads. Like sweets, carbs offer a euphoric spike in blood sugar, often followed by a drowsy crash. Still others suggest that comfort food is food that's high in fat calories—and guaranteed to make us feel warm when it's cold outside. Psychologists suggest that comfort food is that which elicits a warm, positive memory. It needn't be warm; it could actually be something cold that you made with your dad on a hot summer day, like ice cream.

Michael Moss explains in his 2013 book *Salt Sugar Fat* how the twenty-first-century human became addicted to food. The whole thing harks back to when our ancestors were hunters and gatherers. They really needed to consume mega calories and pack on the pounds, just to get the work of living accomplished and to survive lean times on their bodies' reserves. When our ancestors encountered certain high-value foods, the body's message was: consume all you can. We are still genetically predisposed to crave those types of foods.

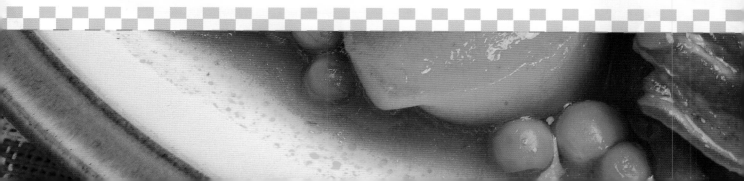

The processed food industry has taken full advantage of our physiological cravings. It calculates a bliss point for most processed foods. That is a point at which more or less sugar, fat, or salt will make us avoid another helping. Moss contends, with scientific backing, that some aspects of food are potentially addicting. And he says that the processed food industry knows that well.

The problem is not so much that we are physiologically and psychologically predisposed to consume certain foods as it is that profiteers use that information to sell us as much as they can—to the detriment of our collective health. But comfort food is not the culprit here.

True comfort food is not formulated to tickle your bliss point, nor is it intrinsically unhealthy. Rather, comfort food is wonderfully delicious and nutritious.

Comfort food is real food. That's food made from scratch using as many whole ingredients as possible. There's nothing so wholesome as whole milk and cream (unless you are allergic to them). Butter, lard, cold-pressed olive oil, coconut oil, and other unadulterated fats are key—steamed asparagus with butter, salt, and pepper is about as comforting as it gets in early spring. Comfort food makes use of real sweeteners such as sugar,

honey, and molasses as needed. Whole grains, fruits, nuts, legumes, fresh vegetables, fresh herbs, meats, seafood, and fish are all part of the comfort food canon. And finally, the emotionally uplifting experiences surrounding the growing, gathering, and processing of ingredients; the making of the dishes; and the sharing of meals all play an important role in creating comfort food.

Grit has celebrated comfort food in its various forms for more than 130 years. The magazine currently devotes many pages of each issue to the sharing of comfort food recipes. We also have a number of recipe-related newsletters, special issues, and websites devoted to high-quality, from-scratch cooking. We've been at it so long that we even have a computer database that contains thousands of comfort food recipes—alongside thousands more in hard copy.

In this book, we celebrate comfort food through recipes gleaned from our archives, current readers, staff members, friends, and family. It offers but a small sample of the treasures, but we think these are the best of the best.

Oscar H. Will III
Editor-in-chief, *Grit*

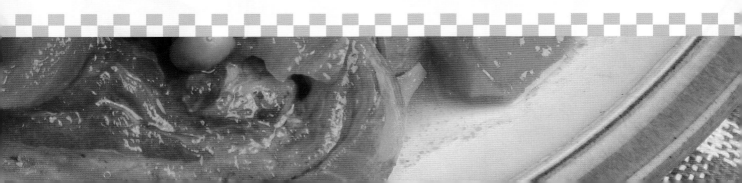

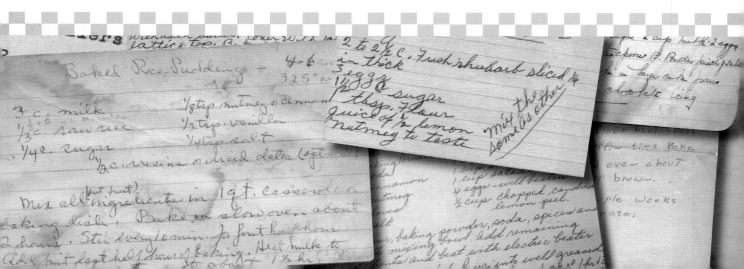

Chapter 1
Breakfasts

THE START OF ANY DAY—especially a day on the farm—is determined by the weather and what we eat for breakfast. In the olden days, farmers needed fuel to motivate and prepare them for a day full of physical labor, from haying the fields and harvesting the crops to feeding the chickens and hogs. Breakfasts consisted of farm-fresh ingredients: eggs from the henhouse, bacon from the larder, and freshly milled grains from the fields. Comfort foods like biscuits and gravy, pancakes, and quiche, lovingly prepared by the woman of the house, filled bellies and warmed hearts.

Whether it's for a day at the office or a day of mowing the back forty, we still need a hearty breakfast every now and again. Find some time to devote to preparing the day's most important meal.

Wholesome foods made from scratch are always on the menu at *Grit*. Whether you're planning a leisurely Sunday brunch, you're crushed for time with a house full of guests, or you're embarking on an ordinary day, you'll find recipes here to suit your needs. Scrumptious, old-fashioned Cinnamon Rolls and Applesauce Doughnuts will set a festive tone for that Sunday brunch. Overnight Bacon Strata is the perfect make-ahead dish when company comes a-calling. Country Cereal and Egg in the Basket are hearty repasts for perfectly plain days at home.

Basic Buttermilk Biscuits

For some, the definition of good country cooking is mastery of the old-fashioned biscuit. The secret to flaky biscuits is to not overmix or overknead the dough. Cut in the butter so you have varying sizes of fat, from pea-sized to quarter-sized. Knead just until the dough sticks together well, stopping before you have a smooth mass. Another trick is to fold the dough over itself after rolling out, roll again, then cut. This creates extra layers—and flakiness—in the biscuits.

MAKES 1 DOZEN

1½ cups unbleached all-purpose flour

½ cup whole-wheat flour

2½ teaspoons baking powder

½ teaspoon baking soda

½ teaspoon salt

2 tablespoons sugar

6 tablespoons unsalted butter

1 cup buttermilk

Heat oven to 400°F. Lightly butter a baking sheet; set aside.

In a large bowl, combine flours, baking powder, baking soda, salt, and sugar. Using a pastry blender, cut butter into the mixture until it becomes coarse meal. Add buttermilk to dry ingredients and mix until just blended. Do not overmix.

Turn the dough onto a floured surface and knead 8 to 10 times. Roll or pat dough to about ¾ inch thick. Using a 2½-inch biscuit cutter, cut out rounds, using all the dough. Gather scraps after cutting, knead together, and cut again. Place rounds of dough on prepared baking sheet.

Bake biscuits in center of oven for about 15 minutes, until golden brown. Cool biscuits for at least 5 minutes before splitting open. These are best served warm with butter and honey, but room temperature is fine, too.

BASIC BUTTERMILK BISCUITS

Karen K. Will

Cloud Biscuits

Using the same basic technique as Basic Buttermilk Biscuits, these biscuits are a little lighter and fluffier due to the addition of an egg. You may add an extra 1 or 2 tablespoons of sugar to the dough to make a sweet biscuit that's delicious piled high with strawberries and whipped cream.

MAKES 2 DOZEN

2 cups unbleached all-purpose flour

1 tablespoon sugar

4 teaspoons baking powder

½ teaspoon salt

½ cup (8 tablespoons) lard or butter

1 egg, beaten

⅔ cup whole milk

Heat oven to 450°F. Lightly grease a baking sheet and set aside.

In a large bowl, sift together the dry ingredients. Using a pastry blender, cut in the lard or butter.

In a small bowl or measuring cup, combine egg and milk; add to flour mixture all at once. Stir just until the dough comes together in a mass. Turn out on a floured surface. Knead 20 strokes. Roll the dough to ¾ inch thick. Cut straight down with a biscuit cutter or floured juice glass. You may chill the dough for 1 to 3 hours, if desired.

Bake 10 to 14 minutes until golden grown. Allow biscuits to cool several minutes before serving.

CLOUD BISCUITS

JJAVA/Fotolia

Sour Cream Biscuits

The dough for these light and fluffy biscuits doesn't hold together as well as some of the other doughs, because it calls for substantially less shortening. The sour cream renders these biscuits quite moist, with a slightly piquant flavor. They stay fresher longer. To reheat leftovers, place them on a baking sheet and heat at 475°F for 5 to 7 minutes.

MAKES 1 DOZEN

2 cups unbleached all-purpose flour

1 teaspoon baking powder

½ teaspoon baking soda

1 teaspoon salt

2 tablespoons butter

⅔ cup sour cream

¼ cup whole milk

Heat oven to 450°F.

In a medium bowl, sift together the flour, baking powder, baking soda, and salt. Using a pastry blender, cut butter into the flour mixture.

Add sour cream and mix; add milk until the dough is soft and light, but not sticky. Knead about 20 strokes. Pat or roll the dough to ¾ inch thick. Using a biscuit cutter or rim of a drinking glass, cut into rounds; or place dough in a square baking dish, unmold, and cut into squares.

Place biscuits on an ungreased cookie sheet. Bake for 12 to 15 minutes until golden brown. Serve warm with jam and butter.

SOUR CREAM BISCUITS

iStockphoto.com/michaelgatewood

Great weekend breakfasts

Weekends meant big breakfasts of eggs, gravy, bacon or sausage, fried potatoes, and the biggest homemade buttermilk biscuits you ever saw smeared with homemade butter and homemade apple butter.

Cheryl L. Owsley
via Facebook

Cinnamon Breakfast Biscuits

Easier to whip up than cinnamon rolls, these breakfast biscuits satisfy a sweet tooth with their delicious icing. Inside are chunks of dried fruit and wheat bran for a dose of fiber. These biscuits make a perfect Christmas (or other holiday breakfast) treat when guests are expecting something special.

MAKES 1 DOZEN

CINNAMON BREAKFAST BISCUITS

iStockphoto.com/George Bailey

1¾ cups unbleached all-purpose flour

¼ cup wheat bran

2 tablespoons granulated sugar

1 tablespoon baking powder

½ teaspoon cinnamon

¼ teaspoon salt

½ cup butter or lard

⅔ cup milk

½ cup mixed dried fruit bits

½ cup sifted confectioner's sugar

2 to 3 tablespoons orange juice, milk, or water

Heat oven to 400°F.

Combine flour, bran, sugar, baking powder, cinnamon, and salt in a large bowl. Using a pastry blender, cut in the butter. Make a well in the center of the dry mixture. Add milk and fruit bits; stir just until moistened.

Turn the dough out onto a floured surface. Quickly knead dough 10 to 12 strokes, or until nearly smooth. Pat or lightly roll the dough to ½ inch thick. Cut with a floured 2½-inch biscuit cutter or into squares, using a sharp knife.

Place biscuits 1 inch apart on an ungreased baking sheet. Bake for 10 to 12 minutes, until golden brown. Transfer biscuits to a wire rack to cool slightly.

Meanwhile, whisk together confectioner's sugar and enough orange juice (or milk or water) to make an icing of drizzling consistency. Drizzle the icing over biscuits; serve warm.

Easy Sausage Gravy

Making gravy is another essential skill for a country cook. Here are some tips:

- Season as you go. You need a lot of pepper for gravy.
- It may look like you're using a lot of milk, but the flour, sausage, and grease will absorb it.
- Keep stirring. You might be tempted to walk away, but stir, stir, and stir until you have gravy.
- When the gravy starts bubbling, it's done. Turn off the heat. It will thicken a bit more as you get the biscuits ready. It's better to have gravy that's a touch on the thin side than a glob of sticky goo.

MAKES 3 CUPS

EASY SAUSAGE GRAVY

iStockphoto.com/wsmah

1 pound pork sausage
¼ to ½ cup unbleached, all-purpose flour
1 quart milk (or more, if needed)
Salt and pepper

In a large skillet, brown sausage over medium heat. Add enough flour to coat the sausage. Stir until it absorbs sausage grease.

Add milk, salt, and pepper, and stir until thickened. If the gravy is too thick, add more milk, a tablespoon at a time.

Seasoned Sausage Gravy

Grit reader Sherry Alward of Caribou, Maine, uses ½ teaspoon sage and a pinch of cayenne instead of nutmeg, poultry seasoning, Worcestershire sauce, and hot pepper sauce. Substitute your favorite seasonings to suit the dish you're serving.

1 pound sausage
2 tablespoons minced onion
6 tablespoons flour
4 cups milk
½ teaspoon nutmeg
¼ teaspoon salt
½ teaspoon poultry seasoning
Dash Worcestershire sauce
Dash hot pepper sauce, such as Tabasco

In a skillet, brown the sausage over medium heat. Add onion and cook until softened, about 2 to 3 minutes.

Drain the sausage, reserving the drippings. Add sausage and 2 tablespoons of drippings back to the skillet, then stir in the flour.

Add milk and stir. Stir in the seasonings, Worcestershire sauce, and hot pepper sauce. Cook, stirring constantly, until bubbling and thickened.

Country Cereal

A big part of life in the country is making do and not letting anything go to waste. This we inherited from our Depression-era parents and grandparents. If you like rice pudding, you'll love this breakfast cereal most likely invented by a frugal housewife as a means for using leftover rice.

SERVES 6

3 cups cooked brown rice

2 cups whole milk

½ cup raisins or prunes, chopped

1 tablespoon butter

1 teaspoon cinnamon

⅛ teaspoon salt

Honey or brown sugar (optional)

Fresh fruit (optional)

Combine rice, milk, raisins, butter, cinnamon, and salt in a saucepan over medium-high heat. Bring to a boil; stir once or twice. Reduce heat, cover, and simmer 8 to 10 minutes or until thickened.

Serve with honey and fruit.

Baked Oatmeal

This is an incredibly easy way to prepare oatmeal, and the finished dish will have a pleasing, crunchy top crust. Serve it in bowls with pats of butter on top and maple syrup or brown sugar on the side.

⅓ cup melted butter

½ cup brown sugar or granulated sugar

1 egg, beaten

2 cups rolled oats

½ tablespoon baking powder

½ teaspoon salt

¾ cup whole milk

1 apple, chopped

½ cup walnuts, chopped

½ teaspoon cinnamon

Heat oven to 350°F. Grease a 2-quart casserole dish with butter and set aside.

In a large bowl, mix butter, sugar, and egg thoroughly. Add remaining ingredients and mix well. Pour mixture into the prepared dish.

Bake for 25 to 30 minutes until hot and golden brown.

Egg in the Basket

This is a classic, simple dish and a fun way to prepare breakfast—a slice of bread with an egg in the middle. Don't cook the dish over high heat, or the bread will burn before the egg is fully cooked. Serve with the round bread cutout for Egg in the Basket with Lid.

SERVES 1

1 slice bread

1 tablespoon butter

1 egg

Salt and pepper

Using a biscuit cutter or glass, cut a 2-inch hole out of the center of a bread slice.

Melt butter in a small skillet over medium heat. Fry the bread slice in butter until lightly golden.

Turn the bread over and break the egg into the center hole. Reduce heat and cook egg to desired doneness. Flip bread and egg over if desired. Season with salt and pepper.

EGG IN THE BASKET

Karen K. Will

Grandfather's treat

I remember my grandpa, who spoke only when he really meant it, telling me that real butter was the "thing to have." He's also the one who taught me to sop up the egg yolk with my toast (or biscuit. Being a city youngster, I used my white toast). And "you got to have a good cup of coffee" to make the meal complete.

Another time I watched him eat almost a whole jar of homemade strawberry jam with a spoon, and he smiled the entire time; it was his first taste of it in decades. He really appreciated a good breakfast.

Heather Black
via Facebook

Toad in the Hole

This is a traditional British dish—sausages cooked in a Yorkshire pudding batter. In England, it's typically served with gravy and vegetables, often mashed potatoes. As an alternative, you can cut the sausage links into ½-inch slices instead of using whole sausages. If you only have frozen breakfast sausage on hand, place them in the dish while it is preheating.

SERVES 4

1 pound fresh pork sausage links

1 cup unbleached all-purpose flour

1 cup whole milk

2 eggs

2 teaspoons baking powder

½ teaspoon salt

Heat oven to 400°F.

In a skillet over medium-high heat, cook the sausages, browning evenly on all sides. Brush an 11x7-inch baking dish with sausage drippings and place in the oven for 15 minutes.

Beat flour, milk, eggs, baking powder, and salt until smooth.

Remove the hot dish from the oven and place the sausages in the pan in a single layer. Pour the batter over the sausages. Bake uncovered until puffed and golden brown, 25 to 30 minutes. To serve, cut into squares.

TOAD IN THE HOLE

iStockphoto.com/abzee

Farmers' Market Omelet

We definitely count omelets as comfort food—especially cheese omelets made with Gouda oozing out with each forkful. Omelets are a tricky dish to get right. The key is not attempting to fold it during the cooking process. That is done as you are sliding it out of the pan and onto the plate. Endless substitutions can be made using this basic recipe. Use your seasonal garden veggies and whatever kind of cheese you have on hand.

SERVES 2

½ cup sliced mushrooms

½ cup thinly sliced yellow summer squash

½ cup thinly sliced zucchini

¼ cup chopped red bell pepper

2 tablespoons plus ¼ cup water, divided

4 eggs

½ teaspoon dried basil leaves

¼ teaspoon garlic powder

2 tablespoons butter, divided

2 teaspoons grated Parmesan cheese, divided

FARMERS' MARKET OMELET

iStockphoto.com/peredniankina

In a 7- to 10-inch nonstick omelet pan or skillet, combine the mushrooms, squash, zucchini, bell pepper, and 2 tablespoons water. Cook and stir over medium heat until water has evaporated and vegetables are crisp-tender, 3 to 4 minutes. Transfer vegetables to a plate and keep warm. Wipe out the pan with a paper towel.

In a medium bowl, beat together the eggs, remaining ¼ cup water, basil, and garlic powder until blended. Heat 1 tablespoon of butter in the omelet pan over medium-low heat until foaming subsides. Tilt the pan to coat bottom with butter. Pour in half of the egg mixture; it should set at the edges in about 30 seconds.

Gently push cooked portions from edges toward the center with a rubber spatula so uncooked eggs can reach the hot pan surface. Continue cooking, tilting the pan and gently moving cooked portions as needed.

When the top surface of the eggs is thickened, place half of the vegetable mixture on the entire surface of the omelet. Sprinkle on 1 teaspoon of Parmesan cheese. Remove from heat and cover for 3 to 4 minutes until the liquid egg is set. Return the skillet to medium-low heat for 30 seconds. Using the rubber spatula, loosen the edges and slide it halfway out onto a plate. Tilt the pan up so the other half of the omelet folds over itself. Place plate in a 200°F oven to keep warm.

Repeat with remaining egg mixture and remaining vegetable mixture to make a second omelet. Serve immediately.

Breakfast Bacon and Cheddar Quiche

A savory custard mixed with bacon, cheddar, and onion is accented with a touch of cinnamon and black pepper, wrapped in a whole-wheat, cream-cheese crust. This isn't a fancy dish with exotic ingredients, but it definitely satisfies the crowd on a special occasion. Folks will be asking for this recipe. For a richer custard, beat in an additional egg yolk.

SERVES 6

Crust:

1 cup whole-wheat flour

8 ounces cream cheese, softened

½ cup butter, cubed

Filling:

3 eggs

1½ cups half-and-half

⅛ teaspoon black pepper

¼ teaspoon cinnamon

½ teaspoon salt

½ cup crumbled fried bacon or chopped cooked ham

2 cups shredded Swiss or sharp cheddar cheese, divided

½ cup minced onion

½ cup broccoli florets

BREAKFAST BACON AND CHEDDAR QUICHE

iStockphoto.com/bhofack2

Heat oven to 375°F.

Place flour in a large bowl. Using a pastry blender, cut in the cream cheese and butter until a coarse meal forms. Gather up dough into a ball and press into a 12-inch pie plate.

In a large bowl, whisk together the eggs, half-and-half, pepper, cinnamon, salt, and bacon; set aside.

Press 1 cup of the cheese into the crust. Sprinkle with the onion and broccoli. Pour the egg mixture over the crust. Sprinkle the remaining 1 cup of cheese over the top. Bake for 30 to 40 minutes, until set.

Blueberry-Stuffed French Toast

No ordinary French toast, this stuffed version makes for a special breakfast. Stale bread is the perfect candidate for this dish, and conveniently, it is less crumbly and easier to stuff than fresh bread. A lazy version of this dish would be two pieces of French toast with fruit like bananas, strawberries, or berries sandwiched in between, topped with butter, maple syrup, and/or powdered sugar.

SERVES 4

Cooking spray

6 eggs

1 teaspoon orange zest

⅔ cup orange juice

3 tablespoons granulated sugar, divided

Pinch of salt

1 cup fresh or frozen blueberries (thawed and drained, if frozen)

8 slices (1¼-inch thick) Italian bread

⅓ cup sliced almonds

Heat oven to 400°F. Spray a large baking sheet with cooking spray.

In a medium bowl, beat the eggs, orange zest, juice, 2 tablespoons of sugar, and salt until well blended. Pour mixture into a 13x9x2-inch baking dish; set aside.

Place the blueberries in a small bowl and toss with the remaining 1 tablespoon of sugar.

With the tip of a sharp knife, cut a 1½-inch wide pocket in the side of each bread slice. Stuff 2 tablespoons of blueberries into each slice. Place filled slices in egg mixture. Let stand, turning once, until egg mixture is absorbed, about 5 minutes on each side.

Arrange bread on the prepared baking sheet; sprinkle with almonds. Bake until golden brown, about 15 minutes, turning slices after 10 minutes. Serve with Blueberry Orange Sauce.

Blueberry-Orange Sauce

MAKES 2 CUPS

3 tablespoons granulated sugar

1 tablespoon cornstarch

⅛ teaspoon salt (optional)

¼ cup orange juice

¼ cup water

1 cup fresh or frozen blueberries

1 cup orange sections

In a small bowl, combine sugar, cornstarch, and salt; set aside.

In a small saucepan, bring orange juice and water to a boil. Add blueberries and orange sections. Return mixture to a boil; cook until liquid is released from fruit, about 2 minutes. Stir in sugar mixture; cook, stirring constantly, until sauce thickens, 1 to 2 minutes. Serve warm.

Overnight Cheesy Egg Casserole

This is a crowd-pleasing potluck dish, and it's easy to boot. You'll need a dozen eggs and time to start preparation the night before. In the morning, just uncover and bake. It's perfect during holidays, when you have houseguests and need a proper breakfast to serve with minimal effort. For variation, toss in a few vegetables of your choice.

SERVES 6 TO 8

OVERNIGHT CHEESY
EGG CASSEROLE

iStockphoto.com/Geo-grafika

8 ounces shredded Monterey jack cheese

1 tablespoon all-purpose flour

8 ounces shredded cheddar cheese

1 pound fully cooked ham, bacon, or sausage, diced or crumbled

1 dozen eggs

1 cup whole milk

Grease a 9x13-inch baking dish and set aside.

In a medium bowl, toss the Monterey jack cheese with the flour; transfer to the prepared dish. Top with cheddar cheese and meat.

Beat the eggs with milk and pour over the ingredients in the dish. Cover and refrigerate overnight.

Remove from refrigerator 30 minutes before baking. Heat oven to 325°F.

Bake uncovered for 45 minutes or until a knife inserted in the center comes out clean. Let stand for 5 minutes before cutting and serving.

Overnight Bacon Strata

A strata is savory make-ahead breakfast casserole that combines the staple ingredients of bread, eggs, cheese, and milk. It's perfectly reasonable to use stale bread for this strata; in fact, it will better absorb the custard that way. This is another convenient, yet elegant way to feed overnight guests in the morning without having to rise at the crack of dawn.

SERVES 6 TO 8

OVERNIGHT BACON STRATA

Karen K. Will

6 eggs

1½ cups whole milk or half-and-half

1 cup shredded cheddar cheese

½ teaspoon dry mustard

1 pound bacon, cut into ½-inch pieces, cooked and drained

8 slices whole-wheat bread, crusts removed, cut into cubes

In a large bowl, beat eggs until foamy. Add milk, cheese, and mustard; mix well. Add bacon and bread cubes, mix well. Turn into an 8-inch-square baking dish, cover, and refrigerate overnight.

Remove from refrigerator and let stand at room temperature for 15 minutes before baking. Heat oven to 325°F.

Bake uncovered for 45 minutes, until a knife inserted in the center comes out clean.

Fried Potatoes Deluxe

The word *deluxe* refers to the simple but indulgent addition of heavy cream. What isn't made better with cream? Serve these crispy, creamy, old-time hash browns with ketchup or hot sauce, applesauce or jam.

SERVES 4

2 tablespoons cream

4 cups raw shredded potatoes

¾ teaspoon salt

¼ teaspoon black pepper

¼ teaspoon paprika

2 tablespoons butter or lard

In a large bowl, combine the cream and potatoes. Add the salt, pepper, and paprika, and mix well.

In a large skillet over medium-high heat, heat the butter or lard until just sizzling. Pour in the potato mixture and spread it evenly over the pan; cover tightly. Reduce the heat to low and cook until browned on the bottom, about 5 minutes. Remove the lid, turn the potatoes and cook, uncovered, until the other side is browned, about 10 minutes.

Transfer to a serving plate and serve immediately.

Sourdough Hotcakes

These hotcakes are unique and scrumptious. They're more like crepes than pancakes. You'll notice there is no addition of flour to this recipe, just the sourdough, and as a result, you'll end up with a somewhat tart, deliciously true sourdough taste. Making these hotcakes is a bit of a science experiment; when you add the baking soda, the batter will fill with thousands of tiny air bubbles and will double in volume.

MAKES 16 5-INCH HOTCAKES

2 cups sourdough

2 tablespoons granulated sugar

3 tablespoons coconut oil, melted and slightly cooled

1 egg

½ teaspoon salt

1 teaspoon baking soda

1 tablespoon warm water

SOURDOUGH HOTCAKES

Karen K. Will

In a large bowl, mix together the sourdough, sugar, oil, egg, and salt; set aside.

Heat the griddle on medium-high heat.

Mix the baking soda in the warm water, then add to the sourdough mixture. Fold batter gently—do not beat or overmix. The sourdough should fill with bubbles and double in size.

Using a ¼-cup measuring cup, immediately begin spooning the batter onto the hot griddle and cook until browned, flipping once. (These hotcakes should be cooked while bubbles are active.)

Serve immediately with butter, maple syrup, honey, or jam.

Buckwheat Pancakes

Contrary to popular belief, buckwheat is not a cereal grain. It's actually a fruit seed from a plant that's related to rhubarb and sorrel. It's gluten-free and a suitable grain substitute for people who are sensitive to wheat. High in magnesium and fiber, buckwheat is truly a health food. Try these hearty pancakes spread with jam or cream cheese.

MAKES 2 DOZEN

1 package (2¼ teaspoons) active dry yeast

¼ cup lukewarm water

2 cups unbleached all-purpose flour

2 cups buckwheat flour

½ teaspoon baking soda

1 tablespoon hot water

⅛ teaspoon salt

1 tablespoon maple syrup or brown sugar

½ cup milk (add more a spoon at a time if needed)

In a large nonmetallic bowl, dissolve yeast in lukewarm water. Add flours and additional water to make a thick batter. Cover and store in the refrigerator overnight.

In the morning, dissolve baking soda in the hot water. Add to the yeast mixture. Stir in salt, syrup, and enough milk to make a thin batter. Stir well.

Heat a griddle or a cast-iron skillet. Using a ¼-cup measuring cup, scoop batter onto hot griddle and fry pancakes until golden.

BUCKWHEAT PANCAKES

Karen K. Will

Whole-Wheat Waffles

Perfect for special-occasion brunches and holidays, fluffy buttermilk waffles are easy to turn out with a waffle maker. If you like a little crunch in your waffles, add about 2 tablespoons cornmeal to the batter. To keep them warm while making enough for the whole family, hold them in a 200°F oven on a wire rack over a baking sheet.

MAKES 15 4-INCH WAFFLES

1½ cups whole-wheat flour

½ cup unbleached all-purpose flour

2 tablespoons granulated sugar

½ teaspoon baking powder

1 teaspoon baking soda

½ teaspoon salt

3 eggs

2 cups buttermilk

⅓ cup coconut oil, melted and cooled slightly

In a large bowl, combine flours, sugar, baking powder, baking soda, and salt.

Separate eggs and beat egg whites until stiff. Set aside. Add egg yolks, buttermilk, and oil to the dry ingredients; stir well. Fold in egg whites.

Pour batter into well-seasoned, preheated waffle iron. Cook until golden brown. Serve with traditional syrups or fresh fruit.

WHOLE-WHEAT WAFFLES

iStockphoto.com/ JMichl

Breakfast for dinner

Most days, breakfast was milk and cereal. On occasion, though, Mom would serve breakfast for dinner, and those meals were much better than ordinary breakfasts. They were Mom's fluffy pancakes or waffles, dripping with syrup, with bacon on the side. And of course there were the versions that consisted of soft scrambled eggs, filled with cheese and sometimes veggies, bacon, or sausage (my dad favored sausage links), and toast warm from the toaster and covered with butter or jam or both.

Jean Teller
Lawrence, Kansas

Johnnycakes

Johnnycakes made from a simple mix of cornmeal, salt, and water were an early American staple food in New England. This recipe is a variation on the traditional cake. It's more like pancakes but still features cornmeal prominently. These are especially tasty when made from homegrown, freshly ground, multicolored heirloom cornmeal.

MAKES 2 DOZEN

1 egg

⅓ cup sugar

¼ cup butter, melted, divided

1 cup milk

1 teaspoon baking soda

1 cup unbleached, all-purpose flour

¾ cup cornmeal

1 teaspoon salt

In a medium bowl, combine egg, sugar, and 1 tablespoon plus 1 teaspoon butter. Stir in the milk and baking soda. Add flour, cornmeal, and salt. Stir just until dry ingredients are moistened. Cover and let stand in a cool place for 30 minutes.

Preheat a griddle or large cast-iron skillet over medium heat. Pour a little of the remaining butter onto the griddle.

Spoon batter by the tablespoonful onto the hot griddle. Brown on one side; turn and brown the other side. Continue making johnnycakes, adding a little butter to the griddle for each batch. Serve with syrup, jelly, or honey.

Homemade Faux Maple Syrup

Pure maple syrup, made from the sap of various maple trees, is prized for its taste and nutrient content; it's high in zinc, iron, manganese, and calcium. You'll pay top dollar for those qualities, but in a pinch you can always experiment with making your own breakfast syrup.

1 cup water

1 cup packed brown sugar

1 cup granulated sugar

1 teaspoon vanilla extract

1 teaspoon maple flavoring

1 tablespoon butter (optional)

In a heavy saucepan, heat water to boiling. Stir in both sugars. Reduce heat and simmer, stirring constantly, until mixture loses cloudy appearance and thickens. Remove from heat and stir in flavorings and butter. Serve warm.

Applesauce Doughnuts

In the old days, doughnuts didn't carry the stigma they do today. Homemade with pure ingredients and fried in lard from the family's hog, they were a Sunday treat after church. Of course, one can't eat doughnuts every day—especially the store-bought varieties with their trans fats and preservatives. Treat your family to these delicious doughnuts that call to mind those apple cider doughnuts so popular at orchards in fall. If you don't have access to pure, nonhydrogenated lard, substitute butter in the dough and peanut oil for frying.

MAKES 3½ DOZEN

Doughnuts:

5 cups unbleached all-purpose flour

4 teaspoons baking powder

1 teaspoon baking soda

2 teaspoons salt

1 teaspoon nutmeg

1 teaspoon cinnamon

¼ cup lard, softened, plus more for frying

1 cup sugar

3 eggs

1 teaspoon vanilla

1 cup applesauce

½ cup buttermilk

Glaze:

¼ cup apple cider

2 cups confectioner's sugar

APPLESAUCE DOUGHNUTS

Karen K. Will

In a large bowl, sift together the flour, baking powder, baking soda, salt, and spices. Set aside.

In a separate large bowl, cream together the lard, sugar, and eggs. Beat in the vanilla, applesauce, and buttermilk. Add the flour mixture, 1 cup at a time, beating the dough smooth after each addition. The dough will be tacky and moist—a cross between quick bread batter and cookie dough. Cover and chill for 1 hour.

Turn the dough onto a lightly floured board and roll out to ⅜ inch thick. Cut into pieces with a 2½-inch doughnut cutter.

In a cast-iron kettle, heat lard to 2 inches deep and 350°F. Using a metal spatula, slide 3 or 4 doughnuts at a time into the lard and fry for 1 minute on each side, until golden brown all over. Remove from the fat with a slotted spoon and drain on paper towels. Bring the lard back to temperature between each batch.

To prepare the glaze, whisk together the apple cider and confectioner's sugar until smooth. After the doughnuts have cooled for 5 to 10 minutes, dip the tops in the glaze.

Cinnamon Rolls

These cinnamon rolls use an old-fashioned, time-honored method of first making a sponge dough, which allows the dough to ferment and build extra flavor before being combined with the rest of the ingredients. These are large, bakery-style rolls, and the buttermilk icing is irresistible.

A decidedly modern trick for slicing the dough roll: Use unflavored, unwaxed dental floss (or cotton sewing thread) to cleanly cut the dough into rounds. This method allows you to slice through the soft dough without squeezing out the filling.

MAKES 1 DOZEN

Rolls:

2¼ teaspoons active dry yeast

1 teaspoon salt

2 cups lukewarm water

8½ to 9½ cups all-purpose, unbleached flour, divided

1 cup granulated sugar

1 cup lard or butter, chilled, plus more for greasing

1 large egg plus 2 egg yolks

½ cup cold water

½ cup butter, softened

¾ cup packed brown sugar

2 tablespoons cinnamon

Icing:

3 tablespoons cream cheese, softened

3 tablespoons buttermilk

1½ cups confectioner's sugar, divided

¼ teaspoon vanilla extract

In a large bowl, combine the yeast, salt, lukewarm water, and 4 cups of flour. With a large rubber spatula, mix together thoroughly; the dough will be very sticky. Cover with plastic wrap and set in a warm place to rise for 2 hours. In a separate large bowl, cream together the sugar and lard; add 2 cups of flour, 1 at a time, stirring well after each addition; mixture will resemble pie dough. In another bowl, beat the egg and yolks with an electric mixer on medium-high speed until foamy, about 1 minute.

Add the cold water to the eggs and stir to combine. Combine the 3 mixtures all at once and beat on low speed until smooth. Add enough flour (up to 2½ cups) to make the dough similar to the consistency of bread dough. Cover with plastic wrap and set in a warm place to rise, about 1½ to 2 hours.

When doubled in size, turn dough onto a floured board and knead until soft and pliable, about 10 minutes, adding up to 1 cup more flour.

Roll out the dough to a 16x12-inch rectangle that's ⅓ inch thick. Using a rubber spatula, spread the butter evenly over the dough. Combine the brown sugar and cinnamon in a small bowl and sprinkle the mixture evenly over the dough.

Grease two 13x9-inch deep baking dishes.

Starting with the long side closest to you, roll up the dough like a jellyroll. Moisten the edge with water to seal the roll.

Cut the roll into 12 equal slices; place 6 rolls, cut side down, close together in each dish. Cover loosely with a flour-sack cloth or tea towel and set in a warm place to rise until doubled, about 1½ to 2 hours.

Preheat the oven to 350°F. Bake both dishes at the same time for 25 to 30 minutes until golden brown; switch positions of the dishes halfway through the baking time. Remove from the oven and let cool on a wire rack for 5 minutes.

To prepare the icing, place the cream cheese, buttermilk, and half the sugar in a large bowl and beat with an electric mixer until smooth and free of lumps. Add the remaining sugar and the vanilla and beat. Using a tablespoon, drizzle the icing evenly over the rolls. Serve warm.

Chapter 2
Soups and Stews

SAVORY, NUTRITIOUS SOUPS AND stews lie squarely within the category of comfort food. On a cold fall or winter day, nothing can satisfy quite like a big pot of soup simmering away on the stovetop or in the slow cooker. Every family has a favorite soup or stew—tomato, chicken noodle, or chili—that has been passed down through the generations and can be recalled by family members as the stuff from which memories are made.

In the following pages you'll find recipes for traditional Irish Lamb Stew, day-after-Thanksgiving blessings-of-the-bird Turkey Soup, and the old standbys: many different kinds of chicken soup, bean soup, chili, and vegetable soup. And let's not overlook the Sweet and Smoky Slow Beef Stew, Baked Potato Soup, Broccoli and Cheddar Soup, and chowders of all types: clam, salmon, ham, and Creamy Corn Summer Chowder.

Bring back the tradition of Sunday supper with these one-pot meals. Gather the family around the kitchen and have fun cooking up the meal, complete with fresh-baked biscuits or rolls and salad fixings fresh from the garden. With the soup pot bubbling away, there'll be plenty of time to catch up on all the family business.

Amish Acres Bean Soup

This no-nonsense, simple bean soup is typical Amish fare. Use the leftover ham bone from a celebratory supper or ask for one at the supermarket meat counter. Play with the type of beans you use and the seasonings to create different variations of this basic soup.

SERVES 6 TO 8

AMISH ACRES BEAN SOUP
Nitr/Fotolia

1 pound soup beans

1 ham bone

½ cup chopped onion

½ teaspoon celery salt

½ teaspoon seasoning salt

Dash garlic salt

Salt and pepper

Place beans in a large bowl and cover with water; soak overnight.

Drain, add fresh water, and cook slowly over medium-low heat with the ham bone for 2 hours. Remove ham bone and set aside to cool.

Add onion, celery salt, seasoning salt, and garlic salt; season with salt and pepper. Trim off meat from cooled ham bone and return ham bits to the pot. Simmer for 1 hour. If the soup is too thick, add more water. Serve immediately.

Deluxe Vegetable Bean Soup

Great Northern beans are luxurious in soup; they're creamy, smooth, and delicious. If preferred, instead of soaking the beans overnight, you can bring them to a boil and cook for 2 minutes. Remove from heat; cover and let stand for 1 hour. Then proceed as directed below.

SERVES 8

1 pound dried Great Northern beans

2½ quarts water

½ cup olive oil

1 large onion, chopped

1 cup finely chopped celery, leaves included

1 cup diced carrots

2 cloves garlic, minced

1 teaspoon oregano

1 cup diced canned tomatoes

3 tablespoons minced parsley

2 teaspoons salt

½ teaspoon dried basil

In a large kettle, cover beans with water and soak overnight. In the morning, bring beans to a boil; reduce heat. Cover and simmer for 1½ hours, adding more water if necessary.

Heat oil in a heavy skillet; add onion, celery, carrots, garlic, and oregano; sauté for about 10 minutes, stirring constantly. Add to beans. Stir in remaining ingredients and cook for 1 hour, or until beans are tender. Serve immediately.

Broccoli and Cheddar Soup

This creamy soup is as delicious as it is nutritious. It's definitely a crowd pleaser, and it's a great way to get kids to eat broccoli. Serve with a hunk of fresh-from-the-oven wheat bread to round out the meal.

SERVES 6 TO 8

2 tablespoons butter

1 yellow onion, chopped

1 large potato, peeled and chopped

4 cups chopped broccoli

2 cups water or chicken stock

½ teaspoon salt

4 cups milk

2 cups grated cheddar cheese

In a large stockpot, melt butter over medium heat. Add onion and sauté until translucent, about 5 minutes. Add potato, broccoli, and water or stock. Reduce heat to low, cover, and simmer until potato is very tender, about 15 minutes.

Purée soup using an immersion blender, or in batches in a blender, until smooth (or if desired, chunky). Return soup to pot. Add salt, milk, and cheese; cover and cook over medium heat, stirring constantly. Heat only until hot and cheese is melted; do not boil.

BROCCOLI AND CHEDDAR SOUP

Ali Safarov/Fotolia

Simple soup is the best

My mother's minestrone is like no other soup. Really, there's not much to it—an assortment of veggies, a few beans, finished off with pasta shells—but it is hands down my favorite comfort food. The secret, like with most great soups, is her homemade stock. She saves all the bones she can—either beef or chicken—in the freezer until she has enough for a batch of stock. She then lets it simmer away for most of the day, filling the house with the most delightful aroma. This is good, honest, simple food, made even better because she takes the time to do it the way her grandmother taught her—from scratch and with love.

Sarah Sinning
Lawrence, Kansas

Roasted Butternut Squash Soup

This winter squash is loaded with beta carotene and vitamin A. Wouldn't you rather eat your vitamins than pop a pill? Make a double or triple batch and freeze this soup for one of those days when you just don't feel like cooking. You'll be so glad you did.

SERVES 4

2 cloves garlic, peeled

1 large butternut squash, halved and seeds removed

Water

3 tablespoons unsalted butter

3 tablespoons olive oil

1 large Spanish onion, diced

Salt and pepper

2 cups heavy cream

Heat oven to 400°F.

Place garlic cloves in cavities of squash halves. Turn squash cut side down on a jellyroll pan; add ⅓ inch of water to pan. Roast until fork tender; check after 30 minutes.

In a soup pot or large kettle, melt the butter with the oil. When the butter starts to foam, add the onion and sauté until translucent, about 5 minutes.

Scoop the pulp and garlic from the roasted squash and add to the soup pot. Season with salt and pepper. Add water to cover; then add the cream. Bring to a simmer and cook for 10 minutes; do not boil. Using an immersion blender, purée the soup until smooth; alternately, purée in batches in a blender. Serve immediately.

ROASTED BUTTERNUT
SQUASH SOUP

vanillaechoes/Fotolia

Vegetable Soup

Use this basic vegetable soup recipe as a template for your own creation. Add your favorite garden vegetables and herbs and spices—dried thyme, rosemary, a bay leaf, garlic, tarragon, and so on. Make the soup creamy by adding a roux or puréeing it partway. It's all up to you.

SERVES 12

VEGETABLE SOUP
Dusan Zidar/Fotolia

2 quarts beef stock

½ cup barley

1 tablespoon parsley

1 cup diced carrots

1 cup diced potatoes

1 cup diced celery

½ cup chopped onion

1 cup peas or green beans

½ cup diced turnips

1 cup shredded cabbage

2 cups canned tomatoes

Salt and pepper

Place beef stock in a large kettle; add barley and cook over medium-high heat for 30 minutes.

Add parsley and remaining vegetables, except tomatoes. Cook until vegetables are just tender. Add tomatoes and season with salt and pepper. Simmer another 5 minutes. Serve immediately.

Surprise Winter Vegetable Soup

Turnips and rutabagas are often overlooked ingredients, but they are certainly the makings of an elegant soup. Slightly sweet, yet starchy, these root vegetables are loaded with a surprising amount of vitamin C.

SERVES 6

1 cup peeled, diced turnips or rutabagas

2½ cups chicken broth or vegetable stock

1 tablespoon butter

1 tablespoon flour

1½ tablespoons chopped fresh tarragon, mint marigold, or other fresh herb or 1½ teaspoons dried herb

½ cup heavy cream

Salt and white pepper

Chopped fresh parsley for garnish

Combine turnips or rutabagas with the broth in a saucepan. Cook over medium-high heat until vegetables are soft. Allow mixture to cool; purée using an immersion blender or standard blender.

In a large, heavy saucepan, melt the butter over medium heat. Stir in the flour and cook for 1 minute, stirring constantly—do not let the butter brown. Add the puréed vegetables and broth, mixing well. Stir in the herbs and cream and season with salt and pepper. Simmer until completely hot, stirring often. Serve topped with fresh parsley.

Diane's Homemade Chicken Soup

This is the soup to make after a roasted chicken dinner. Strip the carcass while it's warm, or just toss the carcass in the refrigerator overnight and strip it the next morning. There is something very satisfying about getting two great meals out of one bird.

SERVES 4 TO 6

Leftover chicken carcass and reserved drippings

4 cups water

2 stalks celery, sliced

2 to 3 carrots, sliced

1 large onion, chopped

2 cloves garlic, chopped

3 cups chicken stock

2 tablespoons minced fresh parsley

1 tablespoon poultry seasoning

Salt and pepper

Strip all the meat off the chicken carcass and place it in a 3-quart pot with the drippings. Add water and heat over high heat.

Add the remaining ingredients and bring to a boil. Reduce heat and simmer until vegetables are tender, about 2 hours. Season with salt and pepper.

Chicken Noodle Soup

Chicken noodle soup is comfort food like no other. When made from scratch, there's no ailment it can't cure. This makes a big pot—enough for a family gathering or to stash away in the freezer for a rainy day.

SERVES 10 TO 12

2 tablespoons olive oil

2 onions, chopped

3 carrots, quartered and sliced

3 ribs celery, sliced

1 whole chicken (6 to 7 pounds), cut into pieces, fat left intact

2 quarts chicken broth or canned low-sodium broth

1 quart cold water, or as much as needed

4 sprigs fresh parsley

3 sprigs fresh thyme

1 bay leaf

2 cups uncooked egg noodles

Salt and pepper

Heat oil in a large pot over medium heat. Add the onions, carrots, and celery; cook, stirring often, until softened, about 10 minutes.

Add the chicken, broth, and enough cold water to cover the ingredients by 2 inches. Bring to a boil; skim off the foam that rises to the surface.

Add parsley, thyme, and bay leaf. Reduce heat and simmer, uncovered, until chicken is tender, about 2 hours.

Turn off heat. Remove the chicken from the pot and set aside to cool. Remove and discard the bay leaf, parsley, and thyme sprigs. Let soup stand 5 minutes. Skim off fat.

Pull chicken from the bones, tearing meat into bite-size pieces; set aside.

Add noodles to the soup pot and cook over high heat until done, about 10 minutes. Stir in the chicken. Season with salt and pepper. Serve hot with fresh-from-the-oven biscuits.

Hearty Chicken and Rice Soup

This is a great soup to make when you just have that little bit of chicken leftover from a big dinner. The lime juice elevates the flavors and gives this dish a Caribbean vibe. Feel free to substitute half the chicken broth with water.

SERVES 8

10 cups chicken broth

1 medium onion, chopped

1 cup sliced celery

1 cup sliced carrots

¼ cup snipped parsley

½ teaspoon cracked black pepper

½ teaspoon dried thyme

1 bay leaf

1½ cups cubed cooked chicken (about ¾ pound)

2 cups cooked rice

2 tablespoons lime juice

Lime slices for garnish

Combine broth, onion, celery, carrots, parsley, pepper, thyme, and bay leaf in a 6-quart Dutch oven. Heat over medium-high heat and bring to a boil; stir once or twice. Reduce heat and simmer, uncovered, 10 to 15 minutes.

Add chicken; simmer uncovered 5 to 10 minutes until chicken is heated through. Remove and discard the bay leaf. Stir in rice and lime juice just before serving. Garnish with lime slices.

HEARTY CHICKEN AND RICE SOUP

Paul Binet/Fotolia

Turkey Soup

We like to call this blessings-of-the-bird soup because after the Thanksgiving feast is over, the big turkey carcass is still blessing us with yet another meal. You'll get a surprising amount of meat off the carcass once it has been stewed for more than an hour, so expect another hearty meal. Serve with leftover rolls or biscuits.

SERVES 8

1 turkey carcass

3 quarts water

1 tablespoon salt

1 bay leaf

2 tablespoons Worcestershire sauce

2 cups sliced celery

2 cups sliced carrots

1 cup sliced onions

1 cup diced white turnips

2 cups diced potatoes

¼ cup chopped parsley

Break the carcass apart and place in a large saucepan. Add water, salt, bay leaf, and Worcestershire sauce; heat until boiling. Reduce heat and simmer, covered, for 1½ hours.

Remove carcass and pull off any remaining meat; discard bones. Return meat to saucepan. Stir in celery, carrots, onions, turnips, and potatoes. Cover and simmer for about 30 minutes, until vegetables are tender. Stir in parsley. Season with additional salt, if desired.

TURKEY SOUP

teleginatania/Fotolia

Union Pacific Chili

This recipe came to us from a reader. It was scribbled on Union Pacific Railroad stationery, and the reader mentioned that the dish was used to feed hungry railroad workers starting in the mid-1800s. There are many variations of this recipe floating around, but the use of beef suet ties it to the 1800s. For a modern substitution, use olive oil or pure lard.

SERVES 10 TO 12

4 pounds lean beef, coarse chopped (chili grind) or ground

2 cloves garlic, minced

½ cup chili powder

½ cup unbleached, all-purpose flour

4 teaspoons (more or less) salt

2 tablespoons cumin

½ cup beef suet

½ cup butter

2 cups diced onion

2 quarts hot water

2 cups tomato puree

3 cups cooked beans (optional)

In a large bowl, combine the beef with the garlic, chili powder, flour, salt, and cumin, using your hands to work ingredients together.

Heat the suet (or oil) and butter in a large, heavy pot over medium-high heat. Add the onion and sauté until soft but not browned, 5 to 10 minutes. Stir in the meat mixture and cook for 20 minutes, stirring often. Add the water and tomato purée. Bring to a boil, then reduce heat and simmer for 1 hour, stirring often.

Stir in the beans, if desired, and cook for 15 minutes longer.

UNION PACIFIC CHILI

Brent Hofacker/Fotolia

White Turkey Chili

The delicious mix of flavors in this white chili will delight everyone—even hardcore red-meat eaters (though they'll never call this dish chili). You won't be able to turn down a second bowl.

SERVES 10 TO 12

1 pound dried small white beans, rinsed and picked over

3 tablespoons olive oil

2 pounds ground turkey

1 large onion, minced

3 cloves garlic, minced

2 cans (4 ounces each) chopped green chilies

1 tablespoon ground cumin

1 tablespoon dried oregano

1 teaspoon ground cinnamon

Pinch of ground red pepper such as cayenne

8 to 10 cups chicken broth

Salt and pepper

3 cups shredded Monterey jack cheese, divided

Prepared salsa for garnish

Sour cream for garnish

Fresh cilantro, minced, for garnish

The night before, place beans in a large pot or bowl, cover with cold water, and let soak overnight. In the morning, drain the beans.

In a large pot, heat oil over medium-high heat and brown the turkey with onion until onion is soft and translucent, about 10 minutes. Stir in the garlic, chilies, cumin, oregano, cinnamon, and red pepper, and sauté for an additional 3 minutes. Add the beans and 8 cups of the chicken broth. Bring to a boil, then reduce heat and simmer until the beans are tender, 2 to 3 hours.

If the beans seem dry at any point of cooking, add additional chicken broth.

Season the chili with salt and pepper. Just before serving, stir in 1½ cups of cheese and cook until melted, 1 to 2 minutes. Ladle the chili into bowls and garnish with the remaining cheese, salsa, sour cream, and cilantro.

Vegetable Chili

This vegetarian chili will please even the vegans—just garnish with fresh cilantro and pepitas (hulled pumpkin seeds) in lieu of the sour cream and cheese.

SERVES 6

1 cup dried kidney beans

8 cups water, divided

3 tablespoons olive oil

2 cups chopped onion

2 cups chopped green bell pepper

2 cloves garlic, minced

1 cup canned diced low-sodium tomatoes

1 cup bulgur

1½ tablespoons chili powder

¼ teaspoon cayenne pepper

½ teaspoon freshly ground black pepper

2 tablespoons ground cumin

1 tablespoon fresh lemon juice

Soak beans overnight in 3 cups water.

Drain the beans and place them in a large saucepan. Add 3 cups fresh water and cook, uncovered, for 1½ hours, until tender. Drain, rinse, and set aside.

In a large pot, heat oil over medium-high heat. Add onion, pepper, and garlic, and sauté 8 to 10 minutes, until vegetables are soft. Add tomatoes, 2 cups water, and bulgur. Bring to a boil, reduce heat, and simmer for 45 to 60 minutes.

Add the cooked kidney beans, chili powder, cayenne, black pepper, cumin, and lemon juice, and cook an additional 10 minutes. Serve immediately. Garnish with sour cream, cheese, and chopped cilantro.

Creamy Summer Corn Chowder

Corn chowder makes our mouths water. Creamy and sweet, resplendent with sweet corn, savory onions, potatoes, and creamy sharp cheddar, this soup can take the place of dessert in our book.

SERVES 6

CREAMY SUMMER
CORN CHOWDER
dolphy_tv/Fotolia

2 tablespoons unsalted butter

2 carrots, scrubbed, diced

3 scallions, white and light green parts, finely chopped

12 ounces red potatoes, scrubbed and cut into small dice (1½ cups diced)

¾ cup chicken stock

2 cups whole milk

2 cups sweet corn kernels (about 8 large ears)

4 ounces sharp cheddar cheese, optional

Pinch coarse salt

Black pepper, freshly ground

Fresh chives, minced, for garnish

In a soup pot, melt the butter over medium heat. Add carrots and scallions. Sauté over medium-high heat until scallions are tender, 3 to 5 minutes. Add potatoes and stock, then bring to a simmer; cover and cook gently until potatoes are fork tender, about 10 minutes.

Stir in the milk and corn and return to a simmer. Cook gently for about 5 minutes. Stir in the cheese until melted. Season with salt and a generous grinding of pepper. Garnish with chives. Serve hot.

Ham and Cheddar Chowder

This hearty chowder is the perfect meal to make with your day-after-Easter ham. Or substitute chicken for the ham, add a teaspoon of dried thyme, and you'll have a country chicken chowder that's sure to please.

SERVES 6

2 cups water

2 large potatoes, peeled and diced to make about 2 cups

½ cup diced carrots

½ cup diced celery

¼ cup chopped onion

1 teaspoon salt

¼ teaspoon fresh ground pepper

White Sauce:

¼ cup butter

¼ cup flour

2 cups milk

2 cups shredded cheddar cheese

1½ cups diced cooked ham

In a large saucepan or soup pot, combine water, potatoes, carrots, celery, onion, salt, and pepper. Heat over high heat to boiling, and cook for 10 to 12 minutes.

To make the white sauce: Meanwhile, in a small saucepan over medium-low heat, melt the butter. Add flour and stir until smooth, about 1 minute. Add milk slowly; cook, stirring constantly, until mixture thickens. Stir in grated cheese; cook and stir until cheese is melted. Add ham and heat through. Remove from heat.

Combine ham mixture with undrained vegetable mixture. Stir until well blended. Serve hot.

New England Clam Chowder

Clam chowder is a restaurant mainstay on Fridays due to an old Catholic requirement to abstain from meat on Fridays. No longer a requirement (except during Lent), the year-round tradition of serving clam chowder on Fridays remains. Make this version at home any day of the week. Note: Traditional New England clam chowder calls for oyster crackers as a thickener instead of flour.

SERVES 4

4 slices bacon, chopped

1 pound (about 3 medium) potatoes, peeled and cut into ½-inch chunks

¼ cup chopped carrot

¼ cup chopped onion

¼ cup finely chopped celery

1½ cups heavy cream

¼ cup all-purpose flour

2 cans (6.5 ounces each) chopped or minced clams, undrained

1 cup milk

½ cup water

½ teaspoon salt

½ teaspoon Worcestershire sauce

¼ teaspoon pepper

Cook bacon in a medium saucepan over medium heat until crisp; drain. Reserve 2 tablespoons bacon fat in the saucepan.

To the saucepan, add potatoes, carrot, onion, and celery. Cook, stirring frequently, for 6 to 7 minutes, or until potatoes are tender.

In a small bowl, combine cream and flour until blended; add to potato mixture. Stir in clams with juice, milk, water, salt, Worcestershire sauce, pepper, and cooked bacon. Reduce heat to medium-low; cook, stirring frequently, for 15 to 20 minutes, or until creamy and slightly thick. Serve hot.

Salmon Chowder

In the Pacific Northwest, salmon chowder often takes the place of clam chowder on menus. This simple preparation makes it easy. Substitute fresh smoked salmon for a gustatory treat.

SERVES 4

4 strips bacon, diced

1 medium onion, finely diced

3 tablespoons flour

3 cups milk

2½ cups boiled, cubed potatoes

1 can (16 ounces) salmon, broken up

In a heavy skillet over medium heat, brown the bacon and onion. Add flour and milk gradually, stirring until smooth.

Add potatoes and salmon; heat to simmering and cook for 10 minutes. Serve hot, garnished with chopped parsley and paprika.

SALMON CHOWDER
JJAVA/Fotolia

Baked Potato Soup

This hearty soup will remind you of a baked potato bursting with sour cream, bacon, and chives. The trick is to cook everything ahead of time, then just toss it all together to make the finished soup. Make this ahead of time and reheat to serve. The flavor improves overnight.

SERVES 8 TO 10

⅔ cup butter

⅔ cup all-purpose flour

7 cups milk

4 potatoes, baked, cooled, peeled, cubed (about 4 cups)

4 green onions, sliced

12 strips bacon, cooked, crumbled

1¼ cups cheddar cheese, shredded

1 cup sour cream

¾ teaspoon salt

½ teaspoon pepper

In a large soup kettle or Dutch oven, melt the butter. Stir in the flour, heat, and stir until smooth. Gradually add milk, stirring constantly, until thickened. Add potatoes and onions. Bring to a boil, stirring constantly. Reduce heat; simmer for 10 minutes.

Add remaining ingredients. Stir until cheese is melted. Serve immediately.

BAKED POTATO SOUP

phofotos/Fotolia

That's enough milk

On the way home from my grandmother's doctor visit, we stopped at a local grocer. The manager asked, "What's the good news, Clara?" My grandmother replied, "The doc says I need to take a milk bath. I need to get enough to fill up the tub."

The grocer kindly asks my grandma, "Would you like that milk pasteurized?"

She responded, "No. Just up to my neck."
True story.

Julia Wise-Sullivan
Topeka, Kansas

Slow Cooker Potato-Cheese Soup

The beauty of this simple, slow-cooked soup is that no water is drained from the vegetables, which allows the vitamins to remain. It's quite comforting to know a nutritious dinner will be waiting for you when you return home from the office.

SERVES 6 TO 8

6 to 8 potatoes, cubed

1 tablespoon chives, chopped

1⅓ cups chopped celery

⅓ cup chopped parsley

½ cup chopped onion

¼ teaspoon paprika

¼ teaspoon celery seed

1 teaspoon summer savory

1 teaspoon salt

2 tablespoons butter

2 tablespoons all-purpose flour

1 cup milk

2½ cups (about 10 ounces) grated cheddar cheese

Chives, sour cream, and bacon bits, as garnish

SLOW COOKER POTATO-CHEESE SOUP

chiyacat/Fotolia

Place potatoes, chives, celery, parsley, onion, paprika, celery seed, summer savory, and salt in a slow cooker; mix gently and add water just to cover. Cover and cook on high for 1 hour; reduce heat to low and cook 4 to 5 hours or until potatoes are done.

In a medium saucepan over medium-low heat, melt the butter; stir in flour. Keep stirring and do not allow the mixture to brown. Stir in the milk; cook, stirring constantly, until mixture thickens. Add cheese and continue stirring until cheese is melted. Turn slow cooker to high; slowly add cheese mixture to cooked potato mixture. Continue cooking until soup thickens.

Cream of Tomato Soup

This creamy tomato soup is as pure and good as it gets. It contains nothing but garden-fresh tomatoes plus a few pantry staples. Off-season, use your own tomatoes or store-bought organic ones. Serve with a grilled cheese sandwich on a rainy day.

SERVES 6

Water

1 quart tomatoes

1 small onion, peeled and sliced (optional)

4 tablespoons butter

4 tablespoons flour

4 cups milk

Salt and pepper

¼ teaspoon baking soda

CREAM OF TOMATO SOUP

mariontxa/Fotolia

Fill a large soup pot about half-full with water; heat to boiling. Wash the tomatoes and score an X in the bottom of each with a paring knife. Drop the scored tomatoes into the boiling water for about 30 seconds. Remove tomatoes with a slotted spoon and place in a bowl of ice-cold water. Peel off the skins; seed and chop peeled tomatoes.

In a saucepan, place tomatoes and onion, if desired. Simmer, uncovered, about 30 minutes.

Meanwhile, in a larger saucepan, melt the butter over low heat. Blend in the flour, stirring constantly. Gradually add milk and continue cooking and stirring over low heat until white sauce thickens. Season with salt and pepper.

Just before serving, strain tomatoes; add baking soda to tomatoes, then stir cooked tomatoes into white sauce. Mix well and serve immediately.

Tomato-Basil Cheddar Soup

We love endless twists on a classic, comforting tomato soup. This one imparts the flavors of the summer garden plus the richness of cheddar cheese and chicken broth. The roasting of the tomatoes beforehand gives this soup a depth of flavor that will have your friends asking for the recipe.

SERVES 8

10 ripe Roma tomatoes

2 tablespoons olive oil

1 tablespoon salt

1 teaspoon black pepper

3 teaspoons dried oregano, divided

1 tablespoon butter

3 cloves garlic, minced

2 large white onions, chopped

¼ teaspoon red pepper flakes

2 cups canned plum tomatoes

2 cups fresh basil leaves

4 cups chicken broth

Cheddar cheese, grated, for garnish

TOMATO-BASIL CHEDDAR SOUP

eflstudioart/Fotolia

Heat oven to 350°F.

Slice the Roma tomatoes lengthwise. In a large mixing bowl, combine olive oil, salt, pepper, 2 teaspoons oregano, and tomato slices; toss well to coat. Place in a shallow baking dish and bake for 40 minutes.

In a Dutch oven, melt the butter and sauté the garlic, onions, and red pepper flakes. Add canned tomatoes, basil, 1 teaspoon oregano, and broth. Add the baked tomatoes. Simmer, uncovered, for 40 minutes. Using a blender or food mill, purée mixture for a few minutes to desired consistency. Serve in soup bowls and top with grated cheese.

Frozen Tomato Soup

This is the recipe to turn to at the end of summer, when you're waist-deep in all kinds of tomatoes from the garden. Make this soup for the freezer and enjoy it in the dead of winter, when your summer garden is a faint memory.

MAKES 6 QUARTS CONDENSED SOUP

FROZEN TOMATO SOUP
Corinna Gissemann/Fotolia

2 gallons chopped ripe tomatoes

2 cups chopped celery, including leaves

3 cups chopped onion

14 bay leaves

14 whole cloves

1 stick butter, melted

½ cup sugar

½ cup flour

6 teaspoons salt

Combine the tomatoes, celery, onion, bay leaves, and cloves in a large kettle. Cook over medium-high heat for 30 minutes. Remove bay leaves. While hot, put through a food mill; discard remaining solids.

In a large bowl, combine melted butter, sugar, flour, and salt. Add to strained tomatoes and boil for 5 minutes, stirring constantly. Remove from heat and set aside to cool. Divide into plastic freezer containers; label and freeze.

To serve: Defrost in refrigerator or microwave and remove from container. Dilute with an equal amount of water. Heat thoroughly.

High praise for Grandma's chili

There is one lesson I learned as a youngster related to chili and my Grandma Mary's kitchen that sticks out above all else. My Grandma Mary was a fine cook—there are few people who put more love into food and got more enjoyment out of cooking for a bunch of hungry mouths than my grandma. But on one occasion, my brothers and I learned a lesson the hard way when in front of my dad, we suggested maybe we might like to go to a local Pizza Hut rather than eat Grandma Mary's chili for lunch. That evening when Dad got home from work, the entire family was pulled out of bed, and we got a stern lesson: You don't ever disrespect your elders and embarrass your grandma by suggesting her cooking isn't quite good enough. I've eaten her chili with high praise every chance since.

Caleb D. Regan
Lawrence, Kansas

Three Sisters Stew

Three Sisters is a common name for squash, corn, and beans, the three main agricultural crops of certain Native American peoples. The three crops are planted close together. The beans climb the cornstalks, and the squash grows beneath both. Enjoy this stew in the fall, using your garden's bounty.

SERVES 10 TO 12

One 2-pound sugar pumpkin or 1 large butternut squash

1 tablespoon olive oil

1 medium onion, chopped

2 cloves garlic, minced

½ medium bell pepper, cut into short, narrow strips

16 ounces canned diced tomatoes, undrained

2 cups cooked pinto beans

2 cups fresh or frozen corn kernels

1 cup vegetable stock or water

1 to 2 small chilies, seeded and minced

1 teaspoon ground cumin

1 teaspoon dried oregano

Salt and pepper

3 to 4 tablespoons minced fresh cilantro

THREE SISTERS STEW

Mario/Fotolia

Preheat oven to 400°F.

Cut the pumpkin in half lengthwise and remove seeds and fibers. Place the halves, cut side up, in a foil-lined shallow baking pan. Cover with foil.

Bake 40 to 50 minutes, until easily pierced with a knife but still firm. When cool enough to handle, scoop out the pulp and cut into large dice. Set aside.

In a soup pot, heat the oil over medium-low heat. Add onion and sauté until translucent, about 5 to 7 minutes. Add garlic and continue to sauté until onion is golden. Add cooked pumpkin, bell pepper, tomatoes, pinto beans, corn, stock or water, chilies, cumin, and oregano. Simmer gently, covered, until vegetables are tender, about 20 to 25 minutes. Season with salt and pepper.

If time allows, let stew stand at room temperature for 1 to 2 hours before serving, then reheat before serving. Just before serving, stir in cilantro. Stew should be thick and very moist, but not soupy; add additional stock or water, if needed.

Sweet and Smoky Slow Beef Stew

This slow-cooked beef stew is just the thing you need on a cool fall or winter night. The brown sugar and smoked paprika combine for a winning sweet-and-smoky combination.

SERVES 6 TO 8

2 tablespoons olive oil

3 pounds beef stew meat

1 yellow onion, finely chopped

3 cloves garlic, minced

4 cups tomato salsa

2 cups beef stock

¼ cup vinegar

½ cup packed brown sugar

3 tablespoons smoked paprika

Heat oil in a large skillet over medium-high heat. Add beef in batches and cook until browned. Transfer to a slow cooker.

Add remaining ingredients to slow cooker, mixing to combine. Cook on High for 6 to 8 hours, until beef is fall-apart tender.

SWEET AND SMOKY SLOW BEEF STEW

Igor Dutina/Fotolia

A helping hand and a great bowl of chili

To help my folks out with medical expenses incurred after my dad had several surgeries a few years ago, some family members organized a benefit soup supper. My dad owned a business in his small hometown, a community where everyone knew everyone, but I couldn't believe how many people showed up—and my dad couldn't even be there, because he was still in the hospital.

When I saw one of Dad's friends put a $100 bill in the donation jar, I looked at him questioningly, and he said, "What? I love chili. Don't think I won't get my money's worth." He didn't, of course, but he did go back for seconds—and thirds. Every time I eat chili now, I think about the love and support shown to my family during a difficult time. It was a true act of wonderful friends and a loving family and community.

Bobbie Lane
Osage City, Kansas

Mushroom Beef Stew with Dumplings

Anything with the word *dumplings* in it qualifies as comfort food. Be prepared to make a second round of dumplings, because in our experience, there are never enough to go around.

SERVES 6 TO 8

MUSHROOM BEEF STEW
WITH DUMPLINGS

Joe Gough/Fotolia

Stew:

¼ cup all-purpose flour

½ teaspoon salt

2 pounds beef stew meat

¼ cup olive oil

3 cups beef stock

3 large potatoes, cubed

1 yellow onion, chopped

2 carrots, sliced

1 pound white mushrooms, sliced

Dumplings:

1 cup all-purpose flour

1 teaspoon baking powder

¼ teaspoon salt

2 teaspoons minced fresh parsley

½ cup milk

Heat oven to 400°F.

To make stew: Place flour and salt in a plastic bag. Add stew meat and shake to coat. Heat olive oil in a large skillet over medium-high heat. Add beef chunks; brown on all sides and transfer to a covered casserole dish. Add stock to the skillet and scrape up browned bits on the bottom. Pour the stock over the meat. Add potatoes, onion, carrots, and mushrooms to meat and stir to mix. Cover and bake for 2 hours, until meat is tender.

To make dumplings: Meanwhile, in a medium bowl, mix together the flour, baking powder, and salt; stir in parsley. Add milk, stirring just enough to moisten flour. Do not overmix.

Remove stew from oven. Uncover and spoon dumpling dough on top of stew, making 6 to 8 dumplings. Return to the oven uncovered and bake for 10 to 15 minutes, until dumplings are golden brown. Serve immediately.

IRISH LAMB STEW

Joe Gough/Fotolia

Irish Lamb Stew

This Irish stew is the perfect Sunday supper. It's traditionally made with lamb, but can be made with beef just as well; use an equal-size chuck roast.

SERVES 8

2½ pounds boneless lamb shoulder

¼ cup all-purpose flour
(plus 2 tablespoons, optional)

2 teaspoons salt

2 teaspoons dry mustard, divided

2 tablespoons bacon drippings

4 small onions, sliced

2 stalks celery, sliced

3 carrots, peeled and sliced

2 medium potatoes, chopped

2 turnips, chopped

¼ teaspoon marjoram

¼ teaspoon thyme

2 cups water (plus 2 tablespoons, optional)

5 ounces frozen peas

2 tablespoons sugar

2 tablespoons vinegar

Cut meat into chunks. In a plastic bag, combine flour, salt, and 1 teaspoon mustard. Place meat in bag and shake to coat. In a large, heavy saucepan or kettle, heat bacon drippings and brown meat on all sides.

Add vegetables, marjoram, thyme, and water. Cover and simmer for about 1½ hours or until meat is tender. Add peas and cook 5 minutes.

In a small bowl, mix sugar, vinegar, and 1 teaspoon mustard. Add to the stew, blending well. If you like a thicker stew, make a paste of 2 tablespoons flour and 2 tablespoons water, blend well. Stir into the stew and blend until thickened.

Chapter 3
Breads, Biscuits, Muffins, and More

THE SMELL OF HOMEMADE bread in the oven brings a deep sense of comfort. When bread is baking, we know that sustenance is forthcoming. It's hard not to eat the whole loaf, fresh from the oven, in one sitting; that's why most bread recipes make two loaves.

Bread of all kinds, from sandwich loaves to muffins, is best when made from scratch from wholesome ingredients. Before the days of supermarkets and artisan bakeries, our grandmothers and great-grandmothers baked bread daily or weekly without a second thought. Don't put off bread baking for special occasions; practice your hand often.

We love the centuries-old tradition of baking day, when the week's baked goods are made in one marathon session. Bread freezes well, so why not take advantage of modern conveniences and set aside some quality kitchen time for home-baked goodness? Our recipes run the gamut from sandwich bread and no-knead artisan style crusty bread, to quick breads like zucchini and banana, to muffins, scones, and rolls. We've even thrown in homemade pizza crust and soft pretzels.

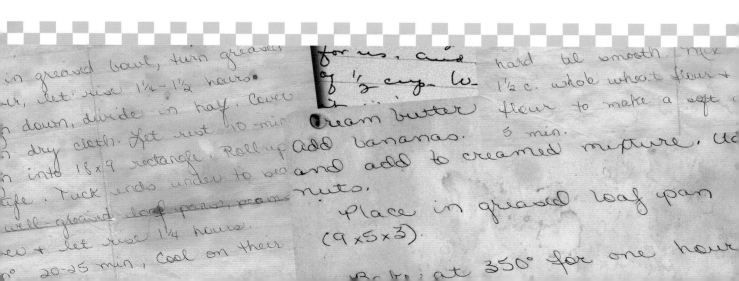

Old-Fashioned White Sandwich Bread

This is the basic white bread our ancestors churned out of their cookstoves and that we grew up eating (and loving). It's made carefully and lovingly, and once you have this method down pat, you will understand the fundamentals of bread baking.

MAKES 2 LOAVES

OLD-FASHIONED WHITE
SANDWICH BREAD

istockphoto.com/PaulCowan

5 cups (25 ounces) unbleached all-purpose flour, divided

1 tablespoon sugar

2½ teaspoons salt

1½ teaspoons quick-rise yeast

2 cups water, room temperature, or 2 cups milk, scalded, then cooled to room temperature

2 tablespoons olive oil or melted unsalted butter

In a large bowl whisk together 2 cups of the flour, the sugar, salt, and yeast. Stir in the water or milk and oil until thoroughly mixed. Stir for 2 minutes, then stir in 2½ cups of flour, ½ cup at a time. The finished dough will be shaggy and sticky. Cover with plastic wrap and let rest for 1 hour at room temperature, then refrigerate for 24 hours.

Remove the dough from the refrigerator and let rest for 1 hour. Scrape the dough out onto a lightly floured (using part of the remaining ½ cup flour) surface. Knead for about 5 or 6 minutes, adding more flour as needed to keep the dough from sticking. Cover the dough with plastic wrap and let rest a few minutes. Clean out the bowl and oil it for a second rise.

Punch down the dough and continue kneading for another 5 or 6 minutes, or until the dough is soft and smooth. Place dough in the oiled bowl, turning to coat all sides. Cover with plastic wrap and set in a warm (82°F is ideal) place to rise until doubled, about 1 hour. (If the house is cool, heat oven to 200°F, allow to heat for 2 minutes, turn it off, and put the dough in to rise.)

Lightly oil two 8½x4½x2½-inch loaf pans. Turn the risen dough out onto a lightly floured surface, flattening gently to break up any large bubbles. Divide the dough into two equal pieces. Press each piece into a 9x12-inch rectangle. Fold in short ends of dough until piece is about 6 inches long. Roll from one rough edge, pinch seam to seal, and roll gently to form a tight log the length of the pan. Place seamside down in prepared pans and press the dough into pans so that it reaches the sides, ends, and corners. Cover the loaves with oiled plastic wrap and let rise for 1 to 1½ hours, or until dough rises just above top of pans and springs back a little when lightly poked with a floured finger.

During the last 20 minutes, heat the oven to 450°F. Put the loaves in the oven and reduce heat to 375°F. Bake for about 45 minutes, or until loaves are golden brown and shrink from sides of pans. Another test is to slip a loaf from the pan and tap it on the bottom—if it's done, it will sound hollow. Remove immediately from pans and let cool on a wire rack for 1 hour. Wrap well as soon as bread has cooled thoroughly. Store at room temperature or freeze in zip-top freezer bags.

Light Wheat Sandwich Bread

This versatile, familiar sandwich loaf is made with honey instead of granulated sugar. Honey is not only more healthful, but it also imparts a unique, earthy flavor to baked goods. You can alter this flavor by choosing different varieties of honey. This bread is springy and will stay fresh longer than bread made with sugar.

MAKES 1 LOAF

1 cup warm water (about 110°F)

2¼ teaspoons active dry yeast

¼ cup honey

½ teaspoon salt

2 tablespoons butter, melted

1 egg

2½ cups unbleached all-purpose flour

1 cup whole-wheat or spelt flour

LIGHT WHEAT SANDWICH BREAD

Karen K. Will

In a large mixing bowl, combine warm water and yeast. Stir and let stand for about 5 minutes, until frothy. Add honey, salt, butter, and egg, and stir well.

In a separate bowl, whisk together the flours. Add most of the flour mixture to the yeast mixture and stir until a ball forms.

Turn out onto a floured surface and knead for 5 minutes, gradually adding remaining flour until it's all incorporated. Place dough in an oiled bowl, turning over once to coat. Cover with plastic wrap and let rise at room temperature for 2 hours.

Turn out dough onto a floured surface and knead for several minutes. Shape into a log and place into a greased (or nonstick) 9x5-inch loaf pan. Press dough evenly into pan, making sure it touches all sides. Cover with plastic wrap and allow to rise again at room temperature for 1 hour.

Heat oven to 400°F.

Once dough has risen and peeks above the pan, bake for 20 minutes. Reduce heat to 350°F and bake for another 17 to 20 minutes, until internal temperature reaches 195°F. Turn out onto a wire rack to cool thoroughly (at least 1 hour) before slicing. Store in a plastic bag.

No-Knead White or Wheat Bread

If you love those expensive, artisan bakery loaves for their thick crusts and moist crumb, start making this no-knead bread at home and save yourself lots of dough. (Sorry.) You will be amazed at just how easy it is to turn out. But keep in mind that you'll need to start your bread the day before you want to bake it. To make wheat bread, substitute ¾ cup whole-wheat flour for bread flour and add 2 tablespoons ground flaxseed, if desired.

MAKES 1 LOAF

NO-KNEAD WHITE OR WHEAT BREAD

Karen K. Will

3 cups bread flour

1¼ teaspoons salt

¼ teaspoon active dry yeast

1½ cups cool water

Coarse cornmeal or wheat bran for dusting

Whisk together all dry ingredients in a large mixing bowl. Add the water and stir with a rubber spatula. Keep mixing until you have a thoroughly mixed, wet, sticky mass of dough. Add more water, 1 tablespoon at a time, if needed. (The dough will not be like any other bread you've made; this will be much wetter and will not form a ball.)

Cover the bowl with plastic wrap and let sit at room temperature, out of direct sunlight, for 12 to 18 hours.

After 12 to 18 hours have passed, the dough should be dotted with bubbles and more than doubled in size. Dust a wooden cutting board with bread flour. Using plastic dough scrapers, scrape the dough loose from the sides of the bowl and turn out onto the board in one piece. The dough will be loose and sticky, but do not add more flour. Dust the top lightly with flour and cover with a clean cotton or linen tea towel. Let the dough rise for another 1 to 2 hours.

About 30 minutes before the second rise is complete, place a 3½- to 5-quart cast-iron Dutch oven (without lid) on a rack positioned in the lower third of the oven. Heat oven to 475°F.

Once the oven has reached 475°F, remove the pot using heavy-duty potholders. (Be very careful; the pot and oven are extremely hot.) Sprinkle about

1 teaspoon coarse cornmeal evenly over bottom of pot. For wheat bread, use wheat bran.

Uncover the dough and, using two plastic dough scrapers, shape dough into a ball by folding it over onto itself a few times. With scrapers, lift dough carefully and let it fall into the preheated pot by slowly separating the scrapers. Dust the top of the dough with coarse cornmeal or wheat bran. Cover and bake for 30 minutes.

After 30 minutes, uncover the pot and continue baking for an additional 15 minutes, until loaf is nicely browned.

Using a sturdy wooden or metal spatula, lift the loaf from the pot and transfer to a cooling rack. Do not slice bread for at least 1 hour; this cooling time completes the baking process and shouldn't be overlooked.

Best Oatmeal Bread

This oaty sandwich bread is light and mildly sweet. Substitute up to ⅓ of the bread flour with whole-wheat or spelt flour for a bit of extra fiber and flavor. Bread flour is used in this recipe because its extra protein (and strength) helps lift the oats and delivers a lighter loaf.

MAKES 2 LOAVES

BEST OATMEAL BREAD

fadzin/Fotolia

5¾ to 6¼ cups bread flour, divided

2½ cups oats, quick or old-fashioned, uncooked

¼ cup granulated sugar

2 packages (0.25 ounce each) quick-rise yeast

2½ teaspoons salt

1½ cups water

1¼ cups milk

¼ cup butter

In a large mixing bowl, combine 3 cups of the flour with the oats, sugar, yeast, and salt; mix well.

In a saucepan, heat water, milk, and butter until warm (120°F to 130°F). Add the liquid to the flour mixture. Using an electric mixer on low speed, blend until just moistened; increase speed to medium and continue beating 3 minutes. By hand, gradually stir in enough remaining flour to make a firm dough.

Lightly oil a large bowl and set aside. Turn the dough onto a lightly floured surface. Knead for 5 to 8 minutes until smooth and elastic. Shape the dough to form a ball; place in the prepared bowl, turning once to coat with oil. Cover with plastic wrap and let rise in a warm place for 30 minutes, until doubled in size.

Grease two 8x4-inch or 9x5-inch loaf pans. Punch down the dough. Cover and let it rest for 10 minutes. Divide dough in half. Shape into two loaves and place in prepared pans. Brush lightly with melted butter and sprinkle with oats, if desired. Cover and let rise in a warm place for 10 to 15 minutes, until nearly double in size.

Heat oven to 375°F. Bake 45 to 50 minutes, until dark golden brown. Remove from pans and cool on a wire rack.

Bread Machine Sunflower Wheat Bread

Released in 1987 at American trade shows, the home bread machine has given us more options for making one of the staples in our diet. If you can't knead dough due to physical limitations or are simply looking for an easier way to make bread, a bread machine will become your best kitchen helper.

MAKES 1 LOAF

¾ cup water

⅓ cup cracked wheat

1 cup skim milk, warmed to 80°F

2½ cups bread flour

½ cup whole-wheat flour

1 teaspoon salt

1½ tablespoons butter, softened

2 tablespoons honey

2 tablespoons sunflower seeds, dry-roasted and salted

½ teaspoon orange zest

1 tablespoon orange juice

2 teaspoons active dry yeast

In a small saucepan, heat water and cracked wheat to boiling; cook, stirring occasionally, over medium-high heat until water is absorbed, about 6 minutes. Cool to 80°F.

Put the wheat mixture into a bread machine, according to manufacturer's directions, along with the milk, flours, salt, butter, honey, sunflower seeds, orange zest and juice, and yeast. Select the whole-wheat cycle and bake on the light setting. Do not use the delayed time cycle. Cool before slicing.

If your bread machine does not have a whole-wheat cycle, after the first knead cycle is completed, reset the machine and start it again. The extra knead cycle is important in whole-wheat bread, because it helps make a lighter loaf.

German Dark Rye Bread

Here's one tip to remember when making rye bread: don't overknead the dough; knead just long enough to hold the dough together and allow the flour to absorb the liquid.

MAKES 2 LOAVES

3 cups unbleached all-purpose flour

¼ cup unsweetened cocoa powder

2 packages active dry yeast

1 tablespoon caraway seeds

2 cups water

⅓ cup molasses

2 tablespoons butter

1 tablespoon sugar

1 tablespoon salt

3 to 3½ cups rye flour

In a large mixing bowl, whisk together the all-purpose flour, cocoa, yeast, and caraway seeds until well blended. In a saucepan, combine water, molasses, butter, sugar, and salt. Heat until just warm (115°F to 120°F). Add the warm liquid to the dry mixture. Using an electric mixer, beat at low speed for 30 seconds, scraping the sides of the bowl constantly. Beat for 3 minutes at high speed.

By hand, stir in enough rye flour to make a soft dough. Turn onto a floured surface; knead until smooth, about 5 minutes. Cover with a tea towel and let rest for 20 minutes.

Punch down the dough and divide in half. Shape each half into a round loaf; place on greased baking sheets or in two greased 8-inch pie plates. Brush the surface of each loaf with oil. Using a sharp knife, slash the tops. Cover; let rise until doubled in size, 45 to 60 minutes.

Heat oven to 400°F. Bake for 25 to 30 minutes, until internal temperature reaches 195°F to 200°F. Remove from pans and cool on wire racks for at least an hour before slicing.

The mystery of the flattened bread dough

I have always baked my own bread, but I went through a troubling time about 15 years ago. The loaves would fall once I got them in the pans. I spent the next month trying to figure out what I was doing wrong. I would tweak the recipe, then wait. The first rise would be great. In the pans the dough would start off great, rising OK, then the next thing I knew: flat. What was I doing wrong?

Well, I found out what I was doing wrong one day when I walked into the kitchen by chance.

My then 5-year-old daughter would sneak into the kitchen when I left and press down the dough, because she thought it was fun to play with the dough. So from that day on she has always punched the dough on the first rise but could not touch the loaves once they reached the pans.

My girls have always been in the kitchen with me, and both have become wonderful cooks. We have some wonderful memories over the years, but we always go back to when Mom couldn't bake a loaf of bread.

Deana Piper
via Facebook

Butterhorn Crescent Rolls

The Midwest's beloved crescent roll doesn't have to pop out of a cardboard tube. Have fun with the kids recreating this beloved roll. You might want to double this recipe if your family loves these as much as ours does.

MAKES 1 DOZEN

BUTTERHORN CRESCENT ROLLS
Steven Miller/Fotolia

¾ cup cottage cheese, at room temperature

1 stick butter, softened

1 cup unbleached all-purpose flour

Combine all ingredients in a large mixing bowl. Using an electric mixer, beat on medium speed until well mixed. Divide the dough into three equal parts and place on a plate or baking sheet; chill in the refrigerator until cold.

Heat oven to 350°F.

Lightly dust a work surface with flour. Roll out the dough to about ⅛ inch thick. Cut into 4-inch triangles. Roll up each triangle, starting with a side and ending with the opposite point. Curve the rolls to shape them like crescents and place on ungreased baking sheets.

Bake for 15 to 20 minutes, until golden brown. Drizzle with powdered sugar icing, if desired, or serve with butter.

Quick and Easy Spoon Rolls

These delicious treats are basically yeast rolls disguised as muffins. They're easy to make, with no fancy shaping or fussing required.

MAKES 2 DOZEN

3¾ cups (18¾ ounces) unbleached all-purpose flour

¼ cup sugar

2¼ teaspoons (1 package) instant yeast

1¼ teaspoons salt

2 cups water

½ cup unsalted butter

1 large egg, lightly beaten

In a large bowl, whisk together the flour, sugar, yeast, and salt. Heat the water and butter together until butter is melted and mixture is 120°F to 130°F. Using a dough whisk or large wooden spoon, stir the liquid into the flour mixture along with the beaten egg until blended. The dough will be very sticky. Cover and let rise until doubled, about 35 to 45 minutes.

Grease two muffin tins and set aside. Punch down the dough gently. With a ¼-cup measure, scoop the dough into the prepared muffin tins, filling two-thirds full (a scant ¼ cup). Let rise, uncovered, 20 to 30 minutes, until dough has risen to the top of the cups. During last 15 minutes, heat oven to 400°F.

Bake for 20 minutes, until rolls are golden brown. Let stand 5 minutes before removing from tins.

Featherbeds (Pan Rolls)

Our mothers always made light and fluffy rolls using potato water, they say, because the starch feeds the yeast, quickening the rise time. Also, the potato water should always be put to use since it holds the nutrients of the potato that was boiled in it.

MAKES 2 DOZEN

¾ cup hot potato water or hot water

⅓ cup sugar

1 teaspoon salt

¼ cup butter

¼ cup warm water

1 package (2¼ teaspoons) active dry yeast

1 egg

½ cup mashed potatoes, lukewarm

4½ cups unbleached all-purpose flour, divided

FEATHERBEDS (PAN ROLLS)

Thomas Perkins/Fotolia

Place the hot potato water into a small bowl and stir in the sugar, salt, and butter; cool to lukewarm. Place the warm water in a large bowl and add the yeast. Stir until dissolved.

To the yeast mixture, add the lukewarm potato-water mixture, egg, mashed potatoes, and 2 cups of the flour; beat until smooth. Stir in enough additional flour to form a soft dough. Turn out onto a lightly floured board and knead until smooth and elastic, about 8 to 10 minutes. Place dough in an oiled bowl, turning to coat all sides. Cover and let rise in a warm place, free from drafts, until doubled in bulk, about 1 hour.

Grease two 9-inch round cake pans and set aside.

Punch down the dough. Turn out onto a lightly floured board and divide in half. Divide half of the dough into 12 equal pieces. Form into smooth balls. Place in one of the prepared pans. Repeat with the remaining half of dough. Cover. Let rise in a warm place, free from drafts, until doubled in bulk, about 45 minutes.

Heat oven to 375°F.

Bake for 20 minutes, until golden brown. Remove from oven and brush lightly with melted butter.

Cheddar Herb Biscuits

These savory, cheesy biscuits are the perfect sidekick to a bowl of hot soup on a chilly fall evening. Use sharp cheddar for a flavor boost and slather the biscuits with the best butter you can get your hands on.

MAKES 1 DOZEN

2 cups unbleached all-purpose flour

2 teaspoons salt

½ teaspoon dried basil leaves

½ teaspoon dried oregano leaves

½ cup butter

½ cup shredded cheddar cheese

¾ cup milk

2 cloves garlic, minced

Heat oven to 425°F. Line a baking sheet with parchment paper and set aside.

In a large bowl, combine the flour, salt, basil, and oregano. Using a pastry blender, cut in the butter until the mixture resembles coarse crumbs. Stir in the cheese.

Combine the milk and garlic. Stir milk mixture into the flour mixture until just combined. Do not over mix.

Using a spoon, drop the dough in 12 equal balls onto the prepared baking sheet. Bake 13 to 15 minutes, until lightly browned. Cool on a wire rack.

Sweet Potato Biscuits

Slightly sweet and very nutritious, these biscuits offer more than starch. For a flavor variation, add a teaspoon of pumpkin pie spice or plain cinnamon to the dough.

MAKES 1 DOZEN

1¼ cups sifted unbleached all-purpose flour

4 teaspoons baking powder

1 tablespoon sugar

½ teaspoon salt

¾ cup cooked, mashed sweet potatoes

¼ cup melted butter

⅔ cup milk

Heat oven to 450°F.

Into a medium bowl, sift flour, baking powder, sugar, and salt together; set aside.

In a large bowl, combine the sweet potatoes and butter. Using an electric mixer, beat thoroughly. Stir in the milk and mix well. Add the dry ingredients and stir until well blended.

Lightly dust a work surface with flour. Roll out the dough to ½ inch thick and cut with a floured biscuit cutter. Place biscuits on an ungreased baking sheet.

Bake for 15 minutes, until golden brown.

SWEET POTATO BISCUITS
Jaimie Duplass/Fotolia

Cornbread

A pot of slow-cooked chili just wouldn't be complete without a big plate of cornbread alongside it. Make a bit of honey butter to serve with it. Place 4 ounces (8 tablespoons or ½ cup) butter in a large bowl. Add ¼ cup honey and whip using an electric hand mixer.

MAKES 9 PIECES

CORNBREAD
Brent Hofacker/Fotolia

1 cup unbleached all-purpose flour

¾ cup finely ground cornmeal

¼ cup sugar

1 tablespoon baking powder

½ teaspoon salt

1 cup milk

1 egg, beaten well

2 tablespoons butter, melted

Heat oven to 400°F. Lightly grease a 9x9-inch baking pan and set aside.

Sift flour with cornmeal, sugar, baking powder, and salt. Add milk, egg, and melted butter, and mix well. Pour into the prepared baking pan.

Bake for 20 minutes until bread springs back to the touch. Allow to cool for 15 minutes; slice into nine 3-inch squares.

Oatmeal Honey Scones

The combination of oatmeal and honey is classic comfort food. Throw in cinnamon, brown sugar, and butter, and all the problems of the day begin to dissolve. These scones make a perfect brunch dish or a light dessert, served with tea.

MAKES 18

¾ cup butter

1 cup packed light brown sugar

¼ cup honey

1 egg

2 tablespoons milk

1½ teaspoons vanilla

3 cups uncooked quick oats

1 cup unbleached all-purpose flour

½ teaspoon baking soda

½ teaspoon salt

¼ teaspoon cinnamon

1 cup raisins

Heat oven to 375°F. Grease two baking sheets.

In a large bowl, combine butter, brown sugar, honey, egg, milk, and vanilla; beat with an electric mixer on medium speed until well-blended. In a separate bowl, combine oats, flour, baking soda, salt, and cinnamon; mix into the creamed mixture on low speed just until blended. Stir in the raisins.

Pat dough into an 8x5-inch rectangle ¾ inch thick; cut into 2-inch triangles. Using a spatula, transfer the triangles to the prepared baking sheets, spacing them 2 inches apart.

Bake one sheet at a time for 10 to 12 minutes, until lightly browned. Do not overbake. Cool for 2 minutes on the sheet; transfer to a wire rack to cool completely.

Raspberry-Lemon Scones

These light and sweet scones are perfect in the summertime, when fresh raspberries are abundant. As they bake, the raspberries release their juice, and it permeates the scones. The key to scones is not overworking the dough. Knead it just enough for it to hold together. Cragginess is charming when it comes to scones.

MAKES 8

Scones:

2 cups unbleached all-purpose flour

¼ cup sugar

2½ teaspoons baking powder

¼ teaspoon salt

⅛ teaspoon nutmeg

½ cup (1 stick) butter, cold, cut into small pieces

½ cup milk

1 egg

1 teaspoon lemon zest

¾ cup fresh raspberries

Topping:

1 tablespoon butter, melted

1 tablespoon sugar

RASPBERRY-LEMON SCONES

istockphoto.com/AntiGerasim

Heat oven to 425°F. Lightly butter a baking sheet and set aside.

In a large bowl, combine flour, ¼ cup sugar, baking powder, salt, and nutmeg. With a pastry blender, cut in the butter until mixture resembles coarse crumbs. In a separate bowl, combine milk with egg and lemon zest; mix well. Add milk mixture to dry ingredients; mix just until dry ingredients are moistened and soft dough forms. Gently stir in raspberries.

Gather dough into a ball and turn out onto a lightly floured surface. Knead gently 8 to 10 times.

Transfer to the prepared baking sheet and pat into a 9-inch circle, ½ inch thick. With a sharp knife, cut through the dough to make 8 wedges; do not separate. Brush tops with melted butter; sprinkle with sugar.

Bake 20 to 22 minutes, until golden brown. Cut through scones; separate wedges and serve warm.

Banana Bread

We don't know a single soul who doesn't love a good banana bread. For the best flavor, be sure to use very ripe, heavily speckled bananas.

MAKES 1 LOAF

1½ cups self-rising flour

1 cup whole-wheat flour

½ teaspoon baking soda

1 teaspoon baking powder

¼ teaspoon salt

3 to 4 ripe bananas

2 eggs

½ cup pure lard or butter

½ cup packed brown sugar

1 teaspoon vanilla extract

½ cup chopped pecans

Heat oven to 350°F. Grease and flour a 9x5x4-inch loaf pan; set aside.

In a large bowl, combine flours, baking soda, baking powder, and salt; set aside. In a separate bowl, mash the bananas; set aside. In another bowl, beat the eggs until light; set aside.

In a large bowl, cream the lard or butter with the brown sugar for 3 minutes. Add vanilla and eggs and mix well. Fold in the mashed bananas and pecans. Add the combined dry ingredients and mix just until moistened. Pour batter into the prepared loaf pan.

Bake 1 hour, or until a toothpick inserted near the center comes out clean. Cool completely on a wire rack before slicing.

BANANA BREAD

annie1961/Fotolia

Zucchini Bread

The best use for zucchini we've ever found is a quick bread. Make this bread in the evening and wait until the next morning to slice—it will benefit from the overnight rest. The moisture will redistribute and the flavors will meld, resulting in a perfectly textured sliced loaf.

MAKES 2 LOAVES

3 eggs

½ cup coconut oil, melted and slightly cooled

½ cup butter, melted and slightly cooled

2 cups brown sugar, packed

3 teaspoons vanilla

1 tablespoon molasses

3 cups zucchini, cooked (microwave it for a few minutes, until soft) and then blended until smooth in a blender or food processor

4 cups unbleached all-purpose flour

1 teaspoon baking soda

¼ teaspoon baking powder

2 teaspoons cinnamon

1 teaspoon pumpkin pie spice

½ cup walnuts or pecans, chopped

Heat oven to 350°F. Lightly grease two 8x4-inch loaf pans and set aside.

In a large bowl, beat the eggs. Add oil, butter, and sugar; beat well. Add vanilla, molasses, and zucchini.

Into a separate bowl, sift flour with baking soda, baking powder, cinnamon, and pumpkin pie spice. Add the dry ingredients to the wet ingredients and mix well. Fold in the nuts and divide the batter between the two prepared pans.

Bake for 45 to 60 minutes, until a toothpick inserted near the center comes out clean. Cool completely on a wire rack.

ZUCCHINI BREAD

Lori Dunn

Breakfast Fruit Muffins

These streusel-topped muffins are quick to make and perfect for when houseguests are hoping for a special breakfast. Substitute fresh raspberries, strawberries, blueberries, peaches, and so on when in season, and up to half whole-wheat flour for variation.

MAKES 1 DOZEN

Muffins:

1 cup oats, quick or old-fashioned, uncooked

1 cup unbleached all-purpose flour

1 tablespoon baking powder

½ teaspoon ground cinnamon

1 cup milk

½ cup mashed ripe bananas (about 1 banana)

½ cup raisins

¼ cup coconut oil, melted and slightly cooled

¼ cup packed brown sugar

1 egg, beaten

Topping:

3 tablespoons brown sugar

2 tablespoons butter

1 tablespoon unbleached all-purpose flour

Pinch of cinnamon

¼ cup chopped nuts

BREAKFAST FRUIT MUFFINS
Barbara Helgason/Fotolia

Heat oven to 400°F. Line 12 muffin cups with paper baking cups; set aside.

In a large bowl, whisk together the oats, flour, baking powder, and cinnamon. Make an indentation in the center of the dry ingredients. Add the milk, bananas, raisins, oil, brown sugar, and egg; mix just until dry ingredients are moistened. Spoon into muffin cups, filling them ¾ full.

Prepare topping: In a small bowl, combine brown sugar with butter, flour, cinnamon, and nuts; sprinkle evenly over the muffins.

Bake 20 to 25 minutes, until a toothpick inserted near the center comes out clean. Cool for 5 minutes in the tin, then transfer to a wire rack to cool completely.

Kansas Wheat Berry Muffins

Kansas is known as both the wheat state and the sunflower state, and Kansans love their homegrown products. These kicked-up blueberry muffins are best made with fresh blueberries, but frozen and defrosted berries can also be used. If you use frozen berries, be sure to drain excess liquid before adding berries to the batter.

MAKES 20

2 eggs

½ cup butter, melted

1 cup sugar

½ teaspoon almond extract

1 cup whole-wheat flour

1 cup unbleached all-purpose flour

1 teaspoon baking powder

½ teaspoon salt

2 cups fresh blueberries, washed and dried

¼ cup sunflower seeds

Heat oven to 400°F. Line muffin tins with 20 paper liners and set aside.

In a large bowl, combine the eggs, butter, sugar, and almond extract; beat until well mixed.

In a separate bowl, whisk together the flours, baking powder, and salt; add to the egg mixture and stir just until moistened. Gently fold in the blueberries and sunflower seeds. Fill the prepared muffin cups ¾ full with batter.

Bake 20 minutes, until golden brown and a toothpick inserted in the center comes out clean. Cool on a wire rack.

KANSAS WHEAT BERRY MUFFINS

Stephanie Frey/Fotolia

Yes, baking soda is important

Once when I was young and inexperienced at bread making, I made banana bread, but I couldn't find any baking powder or baking soda. I couldn't bear the thought of not having my favorite fluffy loaf of heaven. I thought, "Well, I wonder if baking soda is really that important." I made the bread anyway and found out just how important baking soda really is. The bread came out resembling something you might build a tornado shelter out of.

Kellsey Trimble
Topeka, Kansas

Homemade Crispy Pizza Dough

Once you have converted to making your own pizza (rather than having it delivered or heating up frozen pies), you'll never go back. This crust is thin and light and is best when not overloaded with toppings. For extra crunch, substitute ¼ to ½ cup nut meal (almond or hazelnut) for some of the flour. This recipe makes two large pizzas—enough for a family.

MAKES 2 LARGE CRUSTS

2½ cups unbleached all-purpose flour

1½ teaspoons quick-rise yeast

1 teaspoon salt

¾ cup warm water (110°F to 115°F)

2 teaspoons honey

3 tablespoons olive oil

HOMEMADE CRISPY PIZZA DOUGH

Karen K. Will

In the bowl of a stand mixer, combine the flour, yeast, and salt. Stir in the water, honey, and olive oil until combined. Knead for about 6 minutes until the dough is smooth and satiny. Shape the dough into a ball and place in an oiled bowl, turning once to coat all sides. Cover and set in a warm spot to rise for 1½ hours.

Turn the dough out onto a floured work surface. Punch it down and divide into two equal parts. If you do not intend to use both crusts, place the leftover in a plastic bag and refrigerate for up to 2 days; otherwise, freeze for up to 1 month. Leave the dough ball to rest for 10 minutes.

Heat oven and baking stone, pizza pan, or baking sheet to 500°F.

Sprinkle the dough with flour and, based on the baking vessel you're using, roll out to a 9x13-inch rectangle or 12-inch circle about ¹⁄₁₆ inch thick.

Drape the dough over a rolling pin and transfer it to the preheated vessel, carefully unrolling it (and being careful not to burn yourself). Spread the sauce and assemble the toppings quickly.

Bake for 10 to 12 minutes until crust is browned and cheese is bubbling.

Soft Pretzels

The doughy, salty soft pretzels we remember from our youth were eaten with mustard at fairs and carnivals. They take us back to another time and place. Make these in your own kitchen for a child's birthday party or bake sale. For variety, top your pretzels—after boiling, before baking—with any of the following: poppy seeds, sesame seeds, caraway seeds, dried onion flakes, Parmesan cheese, or cinnamon-sugar.

MAKES 8 PRETZELS

Pretzels:

1½ cups warm water

2½ teaspoons active dry yeast

1 tablespoon sugar

3½ cups all-purpose flour

1 tablespoon salt

1 egg

Coarse or kosher salt

Water Bath:

1 gallon water

1 tablespoon baking soda

SOFT PRETZELS

Karen K. Will

In a large bowl, combine the warm water, yeast, and sugar, and let sit for 5 minutes until foamy.

In a separate bowl, combine the flour and salt. Add to the yeast mixture and mix until it comes together. Use your hands to combine into a ball. On a lightly floured work surface, knead the dough for a few minutes until a smooth, sticky dough forms.

Place the dough in an oiled bowl and cover with plastic wrap. Let sit for about 45 minutes.

On a lightly floured work surface, divide the dough into eight equal pieces. Roll each piece into a rope about 18 to 20 inches long. (Don't overflour your hands or the work surface, as this will make it more difficult to roll.) Twist each piece into a pretzel shape by placing the arc of the pretzel at the bottom (closest to you); next, round the two ends so they're facing the arc and twist them around each other; "paste" them to opposite sides of the arc, using a little water if necessary. Place on a baking sheet covered with parchment paper.

Heat oven to 400°F. Combine the waterbath ingredients in a large stockpot and bring to a boil. Once boiling, use a slotted spatula to transfer each pretzel into the water and let boil for 3 minutes, flipping once halfway through. Drain on a cooling rack and transfer parboiled pretzels back to the parchment-lined baking sheet.

Beat the egg with 1 tablespoon water. Brush the egg wash generously over each pretzel and sprinkle with coarse or kosher salt.

Bake for 25 minutes, until golden brown.

Holiday Raisin Stollen

The Midwest is heavily populated with German-Americans. Stollen is their traditional Christmas fruitcake, made with dried fruit and covered with icing. It originated in the fifteenth century. Usually sold in tins, this homemade version will delight everyone—even those who turn up their noses at the mere mention of fruitcake.

Fruitcake:

¾ cup raisins

¾ cup golden raisins

3 tablespoons orange juice

3 cups unbleached all-purpose flour, divided

1 package (2¼ teaspoons) active dry yeast

¼ cup sugar

½ teaspoon salt

½ teaspoon nutmeg

½ cup milk

⅓ cup butter, softened

1 tablespoon grated lemon zest

2 eggs, beaten

Glaze and Topping:

1 cup confectioners' sugar

2 to 3 teaspoons lemon juice

Raisins

Candied fruits

In a bowl, combine raisins and orange juice; set aside to stand for at least 1 hour.

Meanwhile, combine 2 cups flour, yeast, sugar, salt, and nutmeg. In a saucepan, combine the milk, butter, and lemon zest until hot, about 125°F to 130°F. Add liquid to the dry ingredients and stir. Mix in eggs and stir in enough remaining flour to make a soft dough.

Turn out the dough onto a lightly floured surface and knead for 5 minutes. Add raisin mixture and knead until smooth and elastic. Cover with a tea towel and let rest for 10 minutes.

Lightly flour the work surface and roll the dough into an 8x12-inch oval. Fold the dough in half lengthwise to within 1/2 inch of opposite side; press closed. Transfer to a greased baking sheet. Cover and let rise in a warm, draft-free place until almost doubled in size, about 40 minutes.

Heat oven to 375°F.

Bake for 25 to 35 minutes, until browned. Transfer to a wire rack to cool completely.

Meanwhile, make the glaze. Mix confectioner's sugar with enough lemon juice to make of glaze consistency. Drizzle on the bread and garnish with additional raisins and candied fruits. Slice and serve.

Chapter 4
Salads and Sandwiches

THERE'S NOTHING FANCY ABOUT sandwiches and salads, and that's why we love them. As great utilizers of leftovers, salads and sandwiches are just what you need when hungry mouths are impatient for lunch or supper. Open the fridge and pull out any combination of random ingredients—chicken, ham, cheese, tomatoes, mayonnaise—and presto, a meal takes shape. A rummage through the vegetable bin supplies lettuce for a salad or just about everything needed for the classic potato salad.

At *Grit*, we love humble victuals like salads and sandwiches. We've come up with recipes for the great trifecta of classic sandwich salads—egg, chicken, and tuna—as well as a few special recipes like a baked Italian club sandwich, homemade ham roll-ups, and a honey-baked ham-filled grilled cheese sandwich. And of course, you don't need a recipe for the easiest comfort food sandwich ever known—the peanut butter and jelly sandwich.

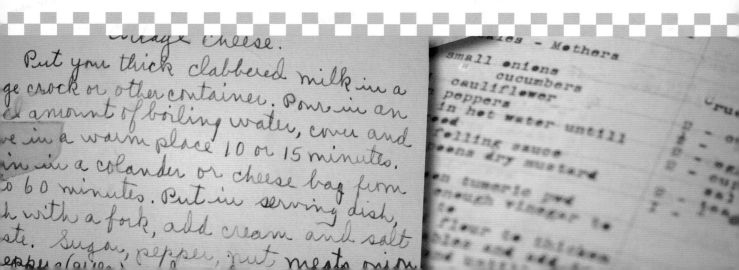

Pasta Cobb Salad

If you love a good Cobb salad, but also love a classic macaroni salad, this one's for you. For a heartier salad, try adding some avocado, tomatoes, green onions, or other garden veggies.

SERVES 6

PASTA COBB SALAD

iStockphoto.com/sbossert

12 ounces small pasta (such as elbows, spiral, or bowtie), uncooked

1 head green leaf lettuce

¾ cup plain yogurt

¼ cup mayonnaise

Salt and pepper (optional)

12 ounces smoked turkey, diced

6 slices bacon, cooked and crumbled

3 hard-boiled eggs, diced

2 celery sticks, diced

1 Granny Smith apple, diced

2 ounces crumbled blue cheese

Cook pasta according to package directions. Drain and rinse with cold water. Set aside.

Separate and trim lettuce leaves; wash and drain. In a food processor or blender, mix yogurt and mayonnaise until smooth. Season with salt and pepper if desired. Set aside.

In a large bowl, stir together the cooked pasta, smoked turkey, bacon, eggs, celery, and apple. Add yogurt mixture and toss gently to coat. Arrange lettuce on six serving plates; spoon pasta mixture onto lettuce. Sprinkle with blue cheese.

Classic Egg Salad

Egg salad is classic because it's one member of the trinity of traditional salads made from high-protein, low carb, and high-fat ingredients. (The other members of the trinity are chicken salad and tuna salad.) This is a basic recipe, but try adding in bacon, cheese, peppers, onions, pickles or pickle relish, and additional spices for variation. Serve this as a salad, as suggested, or on bread or croissants for egg-salad sandwiches.

SERVES 4

CLASSIC EGG SALAD

chas53/Fotolia

6 hard-boiled eggs, sliced

¼ cup mayonnaise

2 teaspoons fresh lemon juice

1 tablespoon minced onion

¼ teaspoon salt

¼ teaspoon black pepper

½ cup finely chopped celery

4 large lettuce leaves

Reserve 4 center egg slices for garnish, if desired. Chop the remaining eggs.

In a medium bowl, mix together the mayonnaise, lemon juice, onion, salt, and pepper. Add the chopped eggs and celery; mix well. Cover and refrigerate for several hours to blend flavors.

To serve, divide evenly among the four lettuce leaves; garnish with reserved egg slices.

Salads need to "bring it"

My father's approach to salads for dinner still sticks with me today. These are not his exact words, but his sentiment was: if a salad wants to make it onto the dinner table as the entrée, it had better "bring it." I'm talking grilled chicken or turkey chunks, ham, mushrooms, eggs, cheddar cheese—it sounds complicated, but it was simple really. Salads needed to have a bunch of meat and vegetables other than lettuce. I still mimic those salads when preparing a salad for dinner.

Caleb D. Regan
Lawrence, Kansas

Classic Chicken Salad

Chicken salad is similar to potato salad in that thousands of recipes and variations exist, as do heated debates over the merits of certain ingredients, like grapes. Chicken salad dates back to 1863, when Liam Gray, owner of Town Meats in Wakefield, Rhode Island, mixed leftover chicken with mayo, tarragon, and grapes.

SERVES 4

2 cups diced, cooked chicken breasts

½ cup thinly sliced celery

⅓ cup thinly sliced, toasted almonds

½ cup seedless red or green grapes, halved

½ cup mayonnaise

2 teaspoons orange juice

1 teaspoon sugar

1 tablespoon milk

¼ teaspoon salt

⅛ teaspoon black pepper

¼ teaspoon poppy seeds (optional)

CLASSIC CHICKEN SALAD

chas53/Fotolia

In a large bowl, combine chicken, celery, almonds, and grapes; set aside.

In another bowl, combine mayonnaise, orange juice, sugar, milk, salt, pepper, and poppy seeds; blend well. Pour over the chicken mixture and toss gently to coat. Cover and refrigerate for several hours before serving.

Serve atop lettuce, on half an avocado, in pita bread halves, or on croissants for sandwiches.

Classic Tuna Salad

Tuna salad is a comforting lunchtime classic, loved for its ease of preparation and use of simple ingredients—what could be easier than grabbing a can of tuna from the pantry? This kicked-up version incorporates some interesting additions. We love the summer savory for its spicy and peppery flavor—it enhances flavor without overpowering it.

SERVES 4

2 tablespoons sour cream

1 tablespoon mayonnaise

2 teaspoons lemon juice

¼ teaspoon summer savory

¼ teaspoon dry mustard

1 teaspoon dried dill

Pinch of black pepper

1 can (7 ounces) tuna, drained and flaked

1 tablespoon chopped onions

½ cup chopped cucumber

¼ cup chopped celery

1 cup chopped seedless grapes

4 large lettuce leaves or 8 thick slices wheat bread

CLASSIC TUNA SALAD

violetapasat/Fotolia

In a large bowl, combine sour cream, mayonnaise, lemon juice, summer savory, mustard, dill, and black pepper; mix well.

Add tuna, onions, cucumber, celery, and grapes; toss gently. Refrigerate for several hours before serving. Serve on lettuce leaves or sturdy wheat bread for sandwiches.

Jell-O-Cranberry Salad

Molded salads are so 1950s, but we all have one or two that we still love to eat. This one isn't molded, but it does call for good old Jell-O. The port wine, walnuts, and creamy topping elevate the flavors to appeal to our twenty-first-century palates.

SERVES 16

Salad:

1 6-ounce package Raspberry Jell-O

1½ cup boiling water

⅔ cup port wine

1 can (20 ounces) crushed pineapple with juice

2 cans (14 ounces) whole cranberry sauce

1 cup chopped walnuts

Topping:

1 8-ounce package cream cheese, softened

1 cup sour cream

½ cup sliced almonds

In a 13x9-inch glass baking dish, pour the boiling water. Using a fork or whisk, blend in the Jell-O, stirring for 5 minutes, until entirely dissolved. Stir in the port. Let set at room temperature for 30 minutes.

Stir in the pineapple, cranberry sauce, and walnuts. Cover and place in the refrigerator for 3 hours or overnight.

To make the topping: Combine the cream cheese and sour cream in a medium bowl. Blend on slow speed until fluffy. Using an offset spatula, carefully spread the topping over the Jell-O mixture. Sprinkle the sliced almonds on top. Cover and refrigerate for several hours before serving. Slice into 16 squares.

JELL-O-CRANBERRY SALAD

Karen K. Will

Mama's Potato Salad

There are as many versions of potato salad as there are stars in the night sky, but the majority of them involve a mayonnaise-based dressing and hard-boiled eggs. Ours—or rather, Mama's—includes the yummy addition of horseradish and capers. Some people like to leave the skins on the potatoes. That's a great idea, because the skins are packed with nutrients. Whatever you do, make this salad the night before you want to serve it, as the flavor improves overnight.

SERVES 10 TO 12

MAMA'S POTATO SALAD

istockphoto.com/DebbiSmirnoff

5 pounds potatoes, red or russet

6 eggs, hard-boiled

1 large onion, chopped

1 clove garlic, minced

1 large cucumber, chopped

2 cups chopped pickles, sweet or dill

½ jar (2½ ounces) capers

1 tablespoon horseradish

1 cup mayonnaise

2 tablespoons prepared mustard

Salt and pepper

2 teaspoons paprika

In large pot, boil the potatoes in enough water to cover. When fork tender, drain and allow to cool. Peel the potatoes and cut into small cubes. Chop the eggs.

In a large bowl, combine the potatoes and eggs. Add the onion, garlic, cucumber, pickles, and capers (if using small capers, leave whole; otherwise chop them).

In a small bowl, mix together the horseradish, mayonnaise, and mustard. Stir into the potato mixture and toss well to coat. Season with salt and pepper. Sprinkle the top with paprika, cover, and refrigerate for several hours before serving.

Dutch Potato Salad

This potato salad comes to us from a Dutch grandmother of the 1950s. It's brilliant in its conservation of ingredients—using the bacon grease as the base for the dressing—and delicious with its flavor combinations. It's a nice departure from the traditional mayonnaise-laden version.

SERVES 4

4 russet potatoes, cleaned and unpeeled

3 slices bacon

2 tablespoons unbleached all-purpose flour

½ cup vinegar

1 tablespoon sugar

¼ cup chopped onion

¼ cup sliced celery

2 hard-boiled eggs, chopped, optional

¼ cup chopped green pepper

Salt and pepper

Place the potatoes in a large pot and cover with water. Boil for 15 to 20 minutes until tender. Drain and cool. When the potatoes are cool enough to handle, peel and slice into ¼-inch pieces.

Fry the bacon until crisp. Remove to a paper towel-lined plate. When cool, crumble into small pieces. To the bacon grease in the pan, add the flour and cook for 3 minutes. Add the vinegar and cook until thin, like the consistency of mustard. Add the sugar and stir until dissolved.

Place the sliced potatoes in a large serving bowl. Add the crumbled bacon, onion, celery, eggs, and green pepper. Season with salt and pepper. Pour on the sauce and toss to coat. Let stand 1 hour at room temperature before serving.

DUTCH POTATO SALAD

Karen K. Will

German Potato Salad

German potato salad, or *Kartoffelsalat*, is traditionally served warm. It's made with vinegar and oil (rather than mayonnaise) and bacon. This recipe marries salty and sweet perfectly with the bacon, vinegar, and sugar. Serve this salad with bratwurst on Christmas Eve.

SERVES 4

2 pounds red or waxy potatoes

Salted water

4 slices bacon

1 small onion, diced

1 cup chopped celery

1 dill pickle, chopped, optional

½ cup water

¼ cup white wine vinegar or cider vinegar

1 teaspoon sugar

1 teaspoon paprika

1 teaspoon dry mustard (optional)

Salt and pepper

Chopped fresh parsley for garnish

GERMAN POTATO SALAD

uckyo/Fotolia

In a large pot, place potatoes and enough salted water to cover; bring to a boil. Reduce heat and simmer, uncovered, for 20 to 25 minutes, until potatoes are fork tender. Drain, peel, and slice. Place warm potatoes in a bowl.

In a skillet, fry bacon until crisp. Drain bacon on paper towels, then crumble and add to the potatoes. Discard all but 2 tablespoons bacon fat. To the skillet, add onion, celery, and pickle. Cook until golden. Add water, vinegar, sugar, paprika, mustard, salt, and pepper; bring just to a boil.

Pour dressing over the potatoes, toss gently to coat, and garnish with chopped fresh parsley.

Garden Patch Potato Salad

This delicious twist on a classic utilizes all your fresh garden vegetables, and to lighten it up a bit, it calls for sour cream rather than mayonnaise.

SERVES 12

8 cups cooked, cubed potatoes

2 cups chopped zucchini

1 cup sliced celery

¾ cup shredded carrots

3 tablespoons finely chopped onion

2 cups sour cream

2 tablespoons vinegar

1 tablespoon sugar

2 teaspoons salt

½ teaspoon dried dill

¼ teaspoon celery seed

⅛ teaspoon black pepper

In a large bowl, combine the potatoes, zucchini, celery, carrots, and onion; set aside.

In a separate bowl, combine the sour cream, vinegar, sugar, salt, dill, celery seed, and black pepper. Mix well and add to the vegetables; toss well to coat.

Press the salad into a 3-quart bowl and refrigerate until needed. Invert on a platter to serve.

Lulu's Sweet Potato Salad

This salad is a lulu because it was sent to us by a woman named Lulu from the Ozarks of Missouri and because it's really good. It's an original Ozark recipe. Serve it chilled with sandwiches, fried chicken, boiled ham, or your favorite barbecued ribs or frankfurters.

SERVES 4

4 medium-sized sweet potatoes, boiled, chilled, diced

½ cup mayonnaise

2 tablespoons lemon juice

¼ cup heavy cream

1½ cups diced celery

3 tablespoons diced sweet pickle

3 tablespoons diced bell pepper

3 tablespoons chopped black walnuts

½ teaspoon salt

Place the sweet potatoes in a large bowl. In a separate bowl, mix together the mayonnaise, lemon juice, cream, celery, pickle, bell pepper, walnuts, and salt.

Pour the dressing over the sweet potatoes and toss to coat. Add more mayonnaise or cream if the salad is too dry. Refrigerate for several hours before serving.

Grilled Spring Asparagus and New Potato Salad

When asparagus spears start to peek up from the soil and baby new potatoes are ready to harvest, fire up the grill. This simple salad enhances the unrivaled, genuine flavor of these two garden delights instead of masking it.

SERVES 6

6 tablespoons extra-virgin olive oil

Juice of 1 lemon

2 cloves garlic, minced

Salt and pepper

1½ pounds new potatoes, halved, or quartered if large

1 pound asparagus, trimmed

12 cups mixed salad greens or mesclun

Freshly grated Parmesan cheese

GRILLED SPRING ASPARAGUS AND NEW POTATO SALAD

istockphoto.com/eyecrave

Prepare a medium fire for a gas or charcoal grill.

In a shallow dish, combine the olive oil, lemon juice, and garlic; season with salt and pepper and mix well. Add the potatoes and asparagus and toss to coat.

In a mesh grill basket or heavy aluminum foil tray, grill the potatoes until golden, about 30 minutes, turning every 10 minutes. Reserve the excess oil and lemon juice mixture.

Grill the asparagus until limp and lightly grill-marked, about 8 minutes.

Arrange salad greens on six individual salad plates. Top with grilled asparagus and potatoes. Drizzle with the remaining olive oil and lemon juice, sprinkle with Parmesan cheese, and serve at once.

Old-Fashioned Ham Salad Spread

This delicious sandwich filling is exquisitely simple. Just combine the ingredients in a food processor and whirl. The very thought of it takes us back to the kitchens of our youth, patiently waiting for lunch to be prepared by Mom or Grandma. But back then, she prepared it the old-fashioned way: by hand.

SERVES 5

OLD-FASHIONED HAM
SALAD SPREAD

MSPhotographic/Fotolia

1 cup cooked ham

¼ cup finely chopped sweet pickles

1½ teaspoons prepared mustard

¼ cup mayonnaise

10 slices white or wheat bread, plain or toasted

In the bowl of a food processor, combine ham and pickles. Pulse for a few seconds. Add mustard and mayonnaise and process just until mixture sticks together.

Spread on bread, add your favorite sandwich fixings—lettuce, pickles, tomatoes—then cut diagonally and serve.

Baked Ham and Cheese Focaccia Sandwich

The aroma of this baked sandwich will conjure an Italian deli in the old neighborhood, with all its authentic meats, cheeses, and antipasto. If focaccia isn't readily available, substitute Italian-style bread by slicing the loaf in half horizontally; scoop out a little bread from the insides to make room for the filling.

SERVES 6

1 12-inch herb-flavored focaccia loaf

6 tablespoons Italian dressing, or oil and vinegar

6 ounces sliced provolone cheese

8 ounces thinly sliced smoked ham

1 jar (7 ounces) roasted red peppers, drained

1 jar (6 ounces) marinated artichoke hearts, drained and sliced

1 teaspoon dried basil

4 ounces sliced mozzarella cheese

Heat oven to 375°F.

With a serrated knife, slice the focaccia horizontally in half. Brush the cut surfaces with Italian dressing. Place bottom layer, cut side up, on a large piece of aluminum foil.

Layer bread with provolone, ham, peppers, and artichoke hearts; sprinkle with basil and top with mozzarella slices. Close sandwich with top half of focaccia. Wrap in aluminum foil.

Bake until sandwich is hot and cheese is melted, about 20 minutes. Cool slightly; cut into wedges to serve.

Cheddary Ham Grill

A grilled cheese sandwich bursting with savory-sweet honey-baked ham is as close to lunchtime perfection as it gets—particularly on a rainy day, with a hot bowl of soup. The orange marmalade and Dijon mustard combine to accent the ham in a really interesting way.

SERVES 1

1 teaspoon orange marmalade

1 teaspoon Dijon mustard

2 slices Italian bread

2 slices sharp cheddar cheese

4 slices smoked or baked honey ham

2 teaspoons butter

In a small bowl, mix together the marmalade and mustard. Spread mixture on 1 slice of bread. Layer cheese and ham over bread; cover with remaining bread slice. Spread outer surface of sandwich with butter.

In skillet over medium heat, grill until lightly browned on both sides.

CHEDDARY HAM GRILL

iStockphoto.com/Lauri Patterson

Easy sandwiches

Grilled cheese sandwiches are easy to make, and I love to bite into the toasty bread and through the gooey cheese. Mom, when she made these for all of us, would use a griddle. I use a small sauté pan, just big enough for one sandwich. And I always use American cheese, because cheddar just doesn't melt properly. Well, not in my mind anyway. And often I'll add bacon—cooked to crispy goodness, added to the sandwich to allow the cheese to melt around the strips.

After I lift the hot sandwich from the pan, I always cut it from corner to corner. There's something special about a sandwich cut on the diagonal; but I never cut off the crusts. That's the best part.

Jean Teller
Lawrence, Kansas

Cheesy Apple and Ham Sandwich

Cheddar and apple is a classic flavor combination. Serve it atop a craggy, buttery English muffin with ham, and you've got a winner. This makes a good breakfast sandwich—with a fried egg in the middle, of course.

MAKES 1 SANDWICH

1 English muffin, toasted

1 tablespoon mayonnaise or butter

1 slice sharp cheddar cheese

3 slices thinly sliced smoked or honey-baked ham

1 Granny Smith apple ring

Ground cinnamon

Layer the muffin half with mayonnaise or butter, cheese, ham, and apple ring. Top with mayonnaise; sprinkle lightly with cinnamon. Top the sandwich with the other half and heat in a toaster oven or microwave, just until cheese melts.

Baked Fresh Tomato, Ham, and Swiss-Filled Rolls

A hot, toasty ham sandwich on a roll is just the thing for a quick, casual supper. When preparing the filling, make sure to dry the tomatoes thoroughly to eliminate excess moisture. Use more or less horseradish according to your taste for the spicy root.

SERVES 4

6 ounces (about 1½ cups) sliced ham, cut into strips

6 ounces (1½ cups) shredded Swiss cheese

2 tablespoons Dijon mustard

1 tablespoon mayonnaise

1 tablespoon prepared horseradish

2 large (about 1 pound) fresh tomatoes, cored and cut into large chunks

4 large round kaiser rolls, cut in half

Heat oven to 400°F.

In a medium bowl, combine ham, cheese, mustard, mayonnaise, and horseradish. Gently stir in the tomatoes; set aside.

Remove the inside from the bottom portion of each roll, leaving shells ½ to ¾ inch thick. Place on a baking sheet. Fill each shell with about 1 cup of ham mixture; top with upper portion of roll.

Bake until heated through and cheese starts to melt, about 15 minutes.

Giant Baked Italian Club Sandwich

When you've got some time and a desire for a real Italian-style sandwich, turn to this recipe. Similar to stromboli, this dish is a real treat. The dough is easy to work and doesn't require rolling like stromboli—just fold it over and seal the edges. Make this for a brunch or special luncheon.

MAKES 2 ROLLS, SERVES 12

Crust:

1 cup warm water

2¼ teaspoons active dry yeast

1 teaspoon honey

2 tablespoons extra-virgin olive oil

3 cups unbleached all-purpose flour

1 teaspoon salt

Filling:

2 tablespoons dry Italian dressing mix

4 tablespoons olive oil, divided

1 onion, thinly sliced

2 tablespoons red wine vinegar

1 clove fresh garlic, minced, or 1 teaspoon garlic powder

½ pound mushrooms, sliced

1 jar (6 ounces) marinated artichoke hearts, drained and sliced

½ pound sliced turkey breast

½ pound sliced ham

½ pound bacon, cooked

2 cups shredded Swiss or jack cheese

Sesame seeds (optional)

To make the dough: In a large bowl, whisk together the water, yeast, and honey. Let sit for 5 minutes until foamy. Stir in the olive oil.

In a separate bowl, mix together the flour and salt. Add half to the yeast mixture and stir to combine. Continue adding the remaining flour until most is incorporated. Turn out onto a floured surface and knead the remaining flour into the dough. Knead an additional 5 minutes until the dough is smooth and tacky. Place the dough in an oiled bowl, turning once to coat. Cover with plastic wrap and set aside to rise for about 1½ hours. Line two baking sheets with parchment paper and set aside.

Meanwhile, combine dressing mix with 2 tablespoons oil; set aside. Heat 1 tablespoon oil in a skillet; add onion and vinegar and cook until onion is translucent. Drain and set aside. Heat remaining 1 tablespoon oil in same skillet; add garlic and mushrooms and sauté until fully cooked. Drain and set aside. Separate leaves of artichoke hearts; pat dry and set aside.

Heat oven to 375°F.

Punch down the dough and divide in half. On a floured surface, roll out each half into a 10x16-inch rectangle approximately ¼ inch thick. Transfer dough to prepared baking sheets. Brush each dough rectangle with half of the dressing mixture. Cover half of the dough lengthwise with turkey, ham, bacon, onion, mushrooms, cheese, and artichoke hearts. Fold dough over filling; seal edges. Cut 3 small slits on top; brush with remaining dressing mixture and sesame seeds if desired. Let rise in a warm place until puffy, about 30 minutes.

Bake for 25 minutes, until golden brown and sounds hollow when tapped. Allow to cool for 5 to 10 minutes before slicing. Cut in half lengthwise; cut crosswise into 2-inch slices.

Ham Roll-Ups

These little sandwich nuggets, when made from scratch with fresh dough, are both special and simple. Don't take a shortcut by using tortillas. Add a slice of cheese and a thin layer of spinach with the ham for a variation.

SERVES 8

1½ cups unbleached
all-purpose flour

1½ teaspoons baking powder

½ teaspoon salt

1 cup shredded cheddar cheese

½ cup butter, softened

¼ cup cold water

8 thin slices boiled ham

Mustard

HAM ROLL-UPS

iStockphoto.com/Lauri Patterson

Heat oven to 450°F. Grease a baking sheet and set aside.

Into a large bowl, sift flour, baking powder, and salt together. Stir in the cheese and butter. Gradually add water, stirring with a fork, until dough sticks together.

Turn out dough onto a lightly floured surface. Knead briefly, about 10 times. Divide dough in half. Roll out each half into a 10x14-inch rectangle. Cut each rectangle into four 5x7-inch pieces.

Place a slice of ham on each piece of dough and spread lightly with mustard. Roll up, jellyroll manner, starting at the narrow end; seal edges. Place the rolls seam side down on the prepared baking sheet.

Bake for 10 to 12 minutes, until golden brown. Remove from oven and cut each roll into 6 slices. Serve hot.

Hot Turkey Sandwich

This is the mother of all day-after-Thanksgiving recipes. A hot turkey sandwich—smothered in gravy and served open-faced on toasted bread—hits the spot when fixing a proper meal is beyond the pale. Utilize other leftovers like stuffing and mashed potatoes, or spread a thick layer of cream cheese on the bread before topping. Yum.

SERVES 4

HOT TURKEY SANDWICH

JJAVA/Fotolia

2 tablespoons butter

2 small carrots, thinly sliced (about ½ cup)

¼ cup sliced celery

1 small onion, peeled and chopped (about ¼ cup)

1½ cups leftover turkey gravy

½ pound turkey, cooked and sliced

4 slices Italian bread, toasted

Whole cranberry sauce (optional)

Melt the butter in a 10-inch skillet over medium heat. Add carrots, celery, and onion, and cook until tender, stirring often. Stir in the gravy and heat through, stirring occasionally.

Arrange the sliced turkey on the bread; ladle gravy mixture over all. Top with a dollop of whole cranberry sauce, if desired.

Classic Club Sandwiches

There's something about the combination of deli meat, bacon, and tomatoes stacked in layers on toasty bread that just screams comfort. Perhaps it reminds us of lunch at a small-town diner while on a family road trip. Omit the turkey, and you've got a great BLT.

SERVES 4

12 slices thin bread, toasted

Butter

8 thin slices roast turkey

4 strips bacon, fried

8 slices tomato

4 leaves of romaine lettuce

2 tablespoons mayonnaise

4 olives

4 pickle spears

CLASSIC CLUB SANDWICHES

3532studio/Fotolia

Butter the toast. For each serving, arrange a slice of toast upon a plate. Cover the toast with 2 slices turkey and top with a crisp bacon strip. Cover with a second slice of toast.

Place a lettuce leaf over the top toast and spread with mayonnaise. Put 2 slices tomato over the lettuce. Finish with a third slice of toast, buttered side down. Fasten with toothpicks and cut into halves. Garnish with a ripe olive and a pickle spear.

BLTs with an extra helping of love

When we were kids, a real treat for us was a BLT made with ripe tomatoes from Dad's garden. What a thrill it was to help Dad pick the tomatoes from the vines, then go inside and help Mom fry up the bacon. Then we'd all sit down at the table, build our delicious BLTs, and talk about anything and everything—the stuff that makes a lifetime of memories.

I've ordered BLTs in restaurants, and I'm always disappointed. They just don't taste the same as they did when I was a youngster. When my family makes them now, they're tasty, but they're still lacking something—I'm pretty sure it's the warm and cozy feeling of sitting around the old kitchen table with Mom and Dad.

Jake Smith
Overbrook, Kansas

Turkey on a Bun

This quick turkey salad is an excellent sandwich filling; stuff it into a leftover dinner roll or hamburger bun and broil it for a minute or two. Add a little cranberry sauce or jam for a flavor kick.

SERVES 6

2 cups diced, cooked turkey

½ cup diced celery

2 tablespoons chopped onion

½ cup shredded cheese

2 hard-boiled eggs, chopped

½ cup mayonnaise

Salt and pepper

Butter

6 hamburger buns or dinner rolls

Heat oven to 400°F.

In a large bowl, combine turkey, celery, onion, cheese, eggs, and mayonnaise; mix well. Season with salt and pepper.

Spread butter on each bun half and fill with turkey salad. Wrap each bun individually in aluminum foil and place on a baking sheet.

Heat for 15 to 20 minutes.

TURKEY ON A BUN

iStockphoto.com/Debbie Smirnoff

Chapter 5
Casseroles

CASSEROLES ARE THE STUFF of legend. From the family dinner table to the potluck buffet, a savory, filling casserole is always a welcome sight. An amalgam of myriad foodstuffs, this beloved invention takes many forms. Cooks take pride in their special combinations of pantry staples and secret-weapon ingredients.

Casseroles became popular in the 1950s, during the height of the convenience food era. Recipes abounded with inexpensive ingredients that were easy to procure: a can of tuna, some fresh or canned vegetables, a can of condensed soup, and a package of pasta or rice. In a short time, dinner was in the oven and the cook could transition to cocktail hour. And here's another reason for casseroles' popularity: they make excellent leftovers. Just cover the dish, refrigerate, and the next day serve it as an encore.

Here at *Grit*, we love a good casserole as much as anyone. We've freshened up some of our recipes, and offer some suggestions for making substitutions. From tuna casserole and lasagnas to cheesy potatoes and turkey tetrazzini, enjoy these dishes of yesteryear. Perhaps take one as a gesture of kindness to someone who is sick or hurting. The recipient will love you for it.

Tuna Casserole

Tuna casserole is present in just about every rural Midwestern potluck spread. Recipes vary slightly, but all claim to have a secret ingredient that makes them better than the rest. Use this recipe as a starting point and add your own flair—a popular sub is crushed potato chips for the bread crumbs.

SERVES 6

2 tablespoons butter

¼ cup chopped onion

¼ cup minced parsley

1 can (6½ ounces) tuna packed in water, drained

1 red or green bell pepper, chopped

1 can (10½ ounces) cream of celery soup

1 cup milk

½ teaspoon salt

1 tablespoon Worcestershire sauce

2 cups small pasta (such as macaroni or spiral), cooked

½ cup bread crumbs

1 tablespoon melted butter

Heat oven to 350°F. Grease a 1½-quart casserole dish and set aside.

In medium saucepan, melt butter. Add onion, parsley, tuna, and pepper, and sauté until onions soften, about 5 minutes. Stir in soup, milk, salt, Worcestershire sauce, and pasta. Mix well.

Place mixture in the prepared dish. Top with bread crumbs and drizzle melted butter on top. Bake 15 to 20 minutes, until casserole is bubbly and bread crumbs are lightly browned.

Monterey Chicken and Rice

This Mexican-inspired casserole has been around for years. It's basic, yet delicious and satisfying. Use leftover roasted chicken or pick up a rotisserie bird on the way home for a quick fix.

SERVES 4 TO 6

2 cups water

1 cup uncooked long-grain rice

1 tablespoon instant chicken bouillon

2 cups sour cream, at room temperature

2 cups cubed, cooked chicken

1½ cups shredded cheddar cheese, divided

1 cup shredded Monterey jack cheese

1 can (4 ounces) chopped green chilies, undrained

½ cup chopped red bell pepper

⅛ teaspoon black pepper

Heat oven to 350°F. Grease a 1½-quart baking dish and set aside.

In a medium saucepan, combine water, rice, and bouillon; bring to a boil. Reduce heat, cover, and simmer for 15 minutes, until rice is tender.

In a large bowl, combine sour cream, chicken, 1 cup cheddar cheese, Monterey jack cheese, green chilies, bell pepper, and black pepper; add cooked rice and mix well. Turn mixture into the prepared dish.

Bake for 20 to 25 minutes. Remove from oven and top with remaining ½ cup cheddar cheese and bake for 3 minutes longer, until melted. Let stand for 5 minutes before serving.

Cheesy Stuffed Shells

You'd be hard-pressed to find anyone who doesn't love this creamy, filling meal. During the fall, we love to add a little puréed pumpkin to the filling (substitute part of the ricotta cheese for it), along with some herbs, like dried thyme or rosemary.

SERVES 8

12 ounces jumbo pasta shells

32 ounces ricotta cheese

2 tablespoons unbleached all-purpose flour

⅛ teaspoon black pepper

⅛ teaspoon nutmeg

3 egg whites

2 cups shredded mozzarella cheese, divided

½ cup grated Parmesan cheese

26 ounces marinara sauce

Heat oven to 350°F.

Cook pasta according to package directions. Rinse with cold water and drain.

Meanwhile, using an electric mixer on low speed, mix together the ricotta cheese, flour, pepper, and nutmeg until blended. Beat in the egg whites. Stir in 1½ cups mozzarella cheese and the Parmesan cheese.

Spread ⅓ of the marinara sauce in the bottom of a roasting pan. Using a small spoon, fill the cooked shells with the cheese mixture and arrange in a single layer in the pan. Pour the remaining sauce over the shells. Sprinkle the remaining ½ cup mozzarella cheese over top.

Bake for 30 minutes, until bubbly.

CHEESY STUFFED SHELLS

Sunny S./Fotolia

Two-in-One Easy Manicotti

Two of our favorite comfort foods—pot roast and manicotti—come together in this recipe. The first night's meal is a classic beef pot roast; the following night's is a delicious baked pasta dish using the leftover roast. The slow-cooked beef makes all the difference in this recipe.

SERVES 4

TWO-IN-ONE EASY MANICOTTI
st-fotograf/Fotolia

Pot Roast:

1 clove garlic, crushed

1 teaspoon dried oregano leaves

½ teaspoon lemon pepper

½ teaspoon salt

1 boneless beef chuck roast (3 to 3½ pounds)

1 tablespoon olive oil

¾ cup water

2 medium carrots

2 medium parsnips

8 small new red potatoes, cut in half

2 small leeks, cut into 1½-inch pieces

2 tablespoons cornstarch, mixed with 1 tablespoon water

Manicotti:

3 cups shredded cooked beef, about 12 ounces

2 to 2½ cups marinara sauce, divided

¼ cup cooking liquid (reserved from beef)

2 tablespoons grated Parmesan cheese

½ teaspoon dried oregano leaves

¼ teaspoon black pepper

6 cooked lasagna noodles, cut in half

½ cup shredded mozzarella cheese

To make the roast: In a small bowl, combine the garlic, oregano, lemon pepper, and salt; press evenly into the surface of the beef roast. In a large Dutch oven, heat the olive oil over medium-high heat until hot. Add the roast and brown evenly on all sides. Pour off the drippings. Add water. Bring to a boil; reduce heat to low. Cover tightly and simmer 1¾ hours.

Cut the carrots and parsnips crosswise into 2½-inch pieces. Cut large ends lengthwise in halves or quarters. Add carrots, parsnips, potatoes, and leeks to the Dutch oven; cover and continue cooking 30 minutes or until the beef and vegetables are tender. Remove the beef and vegetables to a serving platter and keep warm. Reserve ¼ cup of the cooking liquid and set aside. Skim off the fat. Return the cooking liquid to heat and whisk in the cornstarch-water mixture; heat and stir until thickened into gravy. Serve immediately.

Reserve half the roast (about 3 cups shredded beef) and ¼ cup of cooking liquid for the manicotti.

To make the manicotti: Heat oven to 350°F.

In a large bowl, combine beef, ¾ cup sauce, cooking liquid, Parmesan cheese, oregano, and pepper. Spread ¼ cup sauce over the bottom of an 11x7-inch baking dish.

Spread about ¼ cup beef mixture on half of each lasagna noodle. Starting at the short end, carefully roll up each noodle in jellyroll manner. Place seamside down in a single layer on the bottom of the prepared baking dish. Top with the remaining 1 to 1½ cups sauce; sprinkle with mozzarella cheese.

Bake for 30 to 35 minutes, until filling is hot and cheese is melted. Let stand 2 minutes before serving.

Underground Ham Casserole

In this casserole, the ham is underground, or buried under a mountain of mashed potatoes. With 4 quarts (16 cups) of mashed potatoes, this dish feeds a crowd—perfect for your next potluck or family gathering.

SERVES 16 TO 20

4 tablespoons butter

½ cup chopped onions

4 cups cubed, cooked ham

1 tablespoon Worcestershire sauce

2 cans (10½ ounces) cream of mushroom soup

1 cup milk

2 cups cubed cheese

4 quarts mashed potatoes, prepared without salt or milk

1 pint sour cream

1 pound bacon, browned and crumbled

Heat oven to 350°F.

In a large skillet, melt butter over medium heat. Add onions, ham, and Worcestershire sauce, and sauté until onions are tender, 5 to 10 minutes. Turn into a medium to large roasting pan.

In a large saucepan, combine the soup, milk, and cheese; heat gently until cheese melts; pour over the mixture in roasting pan.

In a large bowl, combine the potatoes with sour cream; carefully spread over the casserole in the pan. Top with crumbled bacon.

Bake for 20 minutes, until casserole is bubbling and lightly browned.

Sour Cream Green Beans

Comfort food for kids is often the equivalent of the cook trying to disguise a vegetable with something more appealing, like cheese. This is one of those instances, but the result is one that's loved by kids of all ages. You can serve it as a side dish or double this recipe and make it the main course.

SERVES 2 TO 4

1 can (28 ounces) French-cut green beans (or frozen, same amount)

3 slices bacon

3 tablespoons butter

½ cup minced onion

1 cup sour cream

¾ cup grated Colby or Monterey Jack cheese

Heat oven to 325°F.

In a saucepan, combine beans and bacon and cook over low heat for 30 minutes. In a separate

SOUR CREAM GREEN BEANS
MSPhotographic/Fotolia

saucepan, melt butter over low heat. Add onion and simmer until onions are tender. Add sour cream and heat through.

Pour beans into a 1-quart casserole dish; cover with the sour cream mixture. Top with cheese and bake for 30 minutes.

Cassoulet

Cassoulet is comfort food for many peoples, but especially those who descend from the south of France, where the name originated. In French, a *cassolo* is a deep, round, earthenware pot with slanting sides. This rich, slow-cooked casserole of peasant origins most often contains meat, sausages, and white beans.

SERVES 8

1 tablespoon olive oil

1¼ pounds skinless chicken breast or boneless pork tenderloin, cut into ¾-inch pieces

12 ounces smoked sausage, cut into ½-inch slices

1½ cups chopped onions

1 cup chopped red bell pepper

4 to 6 cloves garlic, minced, divided

1 can (14½ ounces) diced tomatoes

4 cans (15 ounces each) Great Northern beans, rinsed and drained, or 2 cups dry Great Northern beans, cooked

1 teaspoon dried thyme leaves

1¾ cups chicken broth, divided

Salt and black pepper

2½ cups bread crumbs

Heat oven to 350°F.

In a Dutch oven, heat the oil and sauté the chicken and sausage until lightly browned, 8 to 10 minutes. Add onions, bell pepper, and most of the garlic; cook over medium heat for 5 minutes. Stir in tomatoes, beans, thyme, and chicken broth; season with salt and pepper.

Combine bread crumbs and remaining garlic; sprinkle over the bean mixture.

Bake uncovered, until crumbs are browned and beans are thickened, about 1½ hours.

CASSOULET

istockphoto.com/boblin

Eggplant Cheese Bake

Eggplant is a tremendously versatile vegetable, and this dish makes a nutritious and delicious meatless supper. Make two and freeze one for later use.

SERVES 4

1 small eggplant (about 1 pound), peeled and cubed

1 cup Monterey jack cheese, shredded

¾ cup seasoned bread crumbs

2 eggs

1½ cups milk

1 small onion, grated

2 tablespoons chopped parsley

1 teaspoon salt

¼ teaspoon black pepper

1 tablespoon bread crumbs (optional)

1 tablespoon sesame seeds (optional)

Heat oven to 350°F. Grease a 1½-quart casserole dish and set aside.

Place the eggplant in a small saucepan; cover with boiling water and boil 5 minutes. Drain. Add half of the cheese and stir gently until melted. Mix in the seasoned bread crumbs.

In a separate bowl, beat the eggs slightly with milk, onion, parsley, salt, and black pepper; stir into the eggplant mixture. Spoon into the prepared casserole dish.

Sprinkle with the remaining ½ cup cheese and additional bread crumbs and sesame seeds, if desired.

Bake for 40 minutes, until set and golden brown. Serve immediately.

Garden Casserole

If you're in need of a savory and filling casserole chock full of vegetables, this is it. Use a basket full of fresh produce from your garden. Endless variations will work just fine with this recipe. Just use your imagination and whatever you've got on hand.

SERVES 4

1 pound ground beef

Salt and black pepper

3 large potatoes, peeled and thinly sliced

3 large carrots, peeled and thinly sliced

1 large onion, peeled and thinly sliced

1 rib celery, sliced

2 teaspoons caraway seeds

2 teaspoons chopped chives

1 teaspoon garlic powder

2 cans (10½ ounces) cream of mushroom soup

2 cups water

Heat oven to 400°F.

In a skillet, brown the ground beef; drain and reserve drippings; season the beef with salt and pepper.

In a large bowl, mix potatoes, carrots, onion, celery, caraway seeds, chives, and garlic powder. In a 2½-quart casserole dish, alternate layers of meat with vegetables.

In a large saucepan, combine soup with water; season with meat drippings, if desired. Heat, then pour over the casserole.

Bake uncovered for 1 hour.

EGGPLANT CHEESE BAKE

Salvija/Fotolia

Cheesy Potatoes

Here at *Grit*, this popular dish is a staple on our "food days"—a communal potluck whenever the occasion arises. Some cooks use more or less cheddar cheese, some use specifically sharp cheddar cheese. Some use cubed potatoes, while others prefer shredded. This recipe is perfectly suited to adjust to your family's taste.

SERVES 12

2 pounds frozen hash browns, slightly thawed

1 cup (2 sticks) butter, melted, divided

1 pint sour cream

½ cup chopped onion

1 can (10½ ounces) cream of chicken soup

2 cups cheddar cheese

1 teaspoon salt

½ teaspoon black pepper

2 cups crushed cornflakes or bread crumbs

Heat oven to 350°F.

In a large bowl, mix together hash browns and ½ cup (1 stick) melted butter. Add sour cream, onion, soup, cheese, salt, and pepper; mix well. Pour into a 13x9-inch casserole dish.

Mix together cornflakes or bread crumbs and remaining ½ cup melted butter. Spread over top of the potato mixture.

Bake for 1 hour.

CHEESY POTATOES

istockphoto.com/msheldrake

Mashed Potato Casserole

This very simple casserole is a real crowd pleaser. Similar to a loaded baked potato, it's the perfect marriage of flavors and just the thing for a potluck or brunch. It can be made ahead of time and frozen; thaw at room temperature overnight and bake as directed.

SERVES 8

10 medium potatoes, peeled and cooked

Milk (optional)

8 ounces cream cheese, softened

1 cup sour cream

4 strips bacon, cooked and crumbled

½ teaspoon dried minced onion

1 teaspoon garlic salt

½ teaspoon paprika

MASHED POTATO CASSEROLE

msheldrake/Fotolia

Heat oven to 350°F. Grease a 2-quart baking dish and set aside.

In a large mixing bowl, beat the potatoes until smooth; for creamier potatoes, add a small amount of milk; set aside.

In a small mixing bowl, beat the cream cheese and sour cream until fluffy. Add bacon, onion, and garlic salt; stir until well blended. Stir cream cheese mixture into the mashed potatoes and mix thoroughly. Turn mixture into the prepared baking dish. Sprinkle with paprika.

Bake for 30 minutes, until potatoes puff up and begin to brown on the edge.

Cooking with love and plenty of butter

Years ago on my first family vacation with my wife's family, everyone took turns cooking dinner each night. This was a fly-in fishing trip in the middle of Canada, so we were limited on supplies—there wasn't much variety in what we ate day to day. On my day to cook I made pretty much what each of the people before me had prepared, yet everyone was so complimentary about the food. When they asked what I did different, I told them that I made it with love.

In reality I had used about a stick of butter in what I cooked. The secret is long out now so whenever I'm cooking, and adding in butter, someone says, "Look, he's cooking with love."

Bill Uhler
Lawrence, Kansas

Broccoli Cheese Casserole

This is so much more than a basic broccoli-cheese casserole. Loaded with vegetables, this dish can stand up to all kinds of variations. Substitute cauliflower for broccoli; carrots for mushrooms; top with Swiss cheese instead of cheddar; use rice instead of pasta; or add chunks of grilled chicken.

SERVES 8

3 cups broccoli florets

¼ cup water

2 tablespoons olive oil

2 tablespoons butter

1 clove garlic, minced

½ medium onion, minced

3 stalks celery, chopped

2 cups
chopped mushrooms

1 tablespoon unbleached
all-purpose flour

1½ cups whole milk or
half-and-half

Salt and pepper

2 cups grated cheddar
cheese, divided

2 cups pasta (elbow or
rotini) cooked, optional

⅓ cup slivered, roasted almonds, divided

BROCCOLI CHEESE CASSEROLE

Stephanie Frey/Fotolia

Heat oven to 350°F. Butter a 10-inch round or 8-inch square baking dish; set aside.

In a microwave-safe bowl, place broccoli and ¼ cup water. Cover with plastic wrap and microwave on high for 2 minutes; drain.

In a large skillet, heat olive oil and butter over medium heat. Add garlic, onion, and celery. Sauté until vegetables are softened, about 5 minutes. Add mushrooms and continue to sauté until soft, about 5 minutes. Sprinkle flour over vegetables and cook over medium heat, stirring constantly, 2 to 3 minutes.

Stir in milk; season with salt and pepper. Cook until milk thickens, about 2 to 3 minutes. Reduce heat. Add 1½ cups cheese, pasta, ¾ of the almonds, and the broccoli. Stir until cheese is melted and the broccoli is well coated. Pour mixture into the prepared pan. Top with remaining ½ cup cheese and almonds.

Bake for 20 to 25 minutes, until heated through and golden brown on edges. Cover with foil if the casserole is browning too quickly.

Hamburger Casserole with Drop Biscuits

If you love chicken and dumplings (page 118), you'll love this beef version on a cold winter's night when energy reserves need a boost. Protein, fat, and carbohydrates come together in a perfect storm of a casserole.

SERVES 4

4 tablespoons butter or pure lard, divided

3 tablespoons chopped onions

1 pound ground beef

1½ teaspoons salt, divided

Black pepper

1 can (15 ounces) tomato sauce

3½ cups canned green beans, drained

1 cup unbleached all-purpose flour

1½ teaspoons baking powder

½ cup (more or less) milk

Heat oven to 425°F. Grease an 8x8-inch casserole dish and set aside.

In a large skillet, melt 2 tablespoons butter or lard over medium-high heat. Add onions and beef, 1 teaspoon salt, and cook until beef is done. Season with pepper. Add tomato sauce and green beans; blend well. Turn into the prepared casserole dish and set aside.

Sift the flour, baking powder, and remaining ½ teaspoon salt together; cut in the remaining 2 tablespoons butter or lard. Stir in enough milk to make a drop batter, stirring only until flour is moistened. Drop dough by spoonfuls over the casserole.

Bake for 15 to 20 minutes, until biscuits are golden.

HAMBURGER CASSEROLE WITH DROP BISCUITS

Karen K. Will

Hamburger Cheese Bake

For some, childhood memories include the working parent's standby, Hamburger Helper, in its endless iterations. This healthy, homemade baked version with a cheesy tomato sauce will take you back to the days of your youth.

SERVES 6

HAMBURGER CHEESE BAKE
MSPhotographic/Fotolia

4 ounces macaroni

1 pound ground beef

¾ teaspoon salt

⅛ teaspoon black pepper

1 small onion, chopped

1 tablespoon chopped green pepper

¼ teaspoon garlic salt (optional)

8 ounces tomato sauce

½ teaspoon oregano

1 package (3 ounces) cream cheese, softened

¼ cup sour cream

¾ cup cottage cheese

Cook macaroni according to package directions; drain and set aside.

Heat oven to 350°F.

In a large skillet, brown the beef; add salt, black pepper, onion, green pepper, and garlic salt. Stir in the tomato sauce and oregano; set aside.

In a large bowl, blend the cream cheese with the sour cream; stir in cottage cheese and mix well.

Place half of the noodles in an 8x8-inch baking dish. Cover with cream cheese mixture and top with remaining noodles. Pour beef mixture over the top.

Bake for 20 minutes, until bubbling.

Special casserole with special memories

Cooking was not something my dad did very well. However, he did enjoy making one of his favorite casseroles from time to time. Every couple of weeks he would tell Mom to take the night off from fixing supper, that he would take care of it, and he would always make Tater Tot Casserole.

It was actually pretty decent, although Mom did mention a few times that she wished he would learn to make something else. He never did, and now that he's gone, Mom will make it every few months and invite us kids over for supper. Mom's Tater Tot Casserole tastes better than Dad's did, but the memories of Dad fixing supper for the family is what makes the dish so special to all of us.

Sissy Boone
Osage City, Kansas

Cabbage Hamburger Casserole

Being able to work a head of cabbage into a casserole—or any other dish, for that matter—is a cook's delight. Loaded with healthy vitamins, minerals, and fiber, cabbage bulks up a dish. And when paired with meat, vegetables, and cheese, it delivers that stick-to-your-ribs quality that renders any dish comforting.

SERVES 6

1 cup water, divided

1 medium head cabbage, shredded

5 tablespoons butter, divided

½ pound ground beef

¼ cup chopped green pepper

1 medium onion, chopped

2 tablespoons unbleached, all-purpose flour

½ cup whole milk

½ cup grated mild cheddar cheese

1 teaspoon salt

⅛ teaspoon black pepper

½ cup bread crumbs

In a large saucepan, place ½ cup of water and the cabbage. Bring to a boil and cook for 7 minutes; set aside.

Heat oven to 375°F. Grease a 2-quart casserole dish and set aside.

In a large skillet, melt 2 tablespoons of butter. Add the beef and brown with the green peppers and onions; set aside.

Melt 2 tablespoons of butter in a saucepan; add the flour and stir constantly until smooth for 2 minutes. Add milk and remaining ½ cup water; cook until thickened. Add cheese, salt, and pepper; stir until cheese is melted.

In the prepared dish, spread half of the cabbage in the bottom. Layer in half of the beef mixture, and half of the cheese sauce; repeat layers.

In a small bowl, melt the remaining 1 tablespoon of butter in the microwave and stir in the bread crumbs. Mix well and sprinkle over the casserole.

Bake for 20 minutes until heated through and until the bread crumbs are golden.

Dad's bachelor casserole

Nowadays, my casserole encounters are a little more developed than when I was a boy. My wife is darn-good at shepherd's pie, a cheeseburger pasta casserole, and others. But when I was a kid, my dad had a much more simple casserole. I'm pretty sure it was his only bachelor recipe that made the cut and got to the family dining table.

Raw diced potatoes on the bottom of the pan, 1 can drained corn, browned hamburger on top. Open a can of tomato soup, add 1 tablespoon Worcestershire—goodness, he loved that stuff—and mix, then pour over browned hamburger. Bake at 350°F about 45 minutes to 1 hour, and season hamburger with salt, pepper, and onion powder as it bakes. So simple, but it was so good. Years later I'd re-create it as a young bachelor myself.

Caleb D. Regan
Lawrence, Kansas

Riley's Lasagna

Riley is one of our readers. She runs a small-town diner in the Midwest, and she proudly shares her best comfort food recipes with us. Nothing can compete with her classic lasagna for supper. The generous spices and sauce create a rich, intensely flavorful dish that satisfies hungry mouths.

SERVES 8 TO 10

RILEY'S LASAGNA

stevem/Fotolia

1 pound ground beef, browned and drained

1 quart (4 cups) puréed tomatoes, fresh or canned

1 can (6 ounces) tomato paste

2 tablespoons chopped parsley, dried or fresh, divided

1 tablespoon dried basil or 2 tablespoons fresh

1½ teaspoons salt, divided

3 cups cottage cheese

½ teaspoon garlic salt or powder

2 eggs

⅛ teaspoon black pepper

¼ cup grated Parmesan cheese

12 ounces shredded mozzarella cheese

12 uncooked lasagna noodles

Heat oven to 400°F.

In a large bowl, combine the ground beef, tomatoes, tomato paste, 1 tablespoon parsley, basil, and ½ teaspoon salt.

In a separate bowl, combine the cottage cheese, garlic salt, eggs, black pepper, Parmesan, remaining 1 teaspoon salt, and remaining 1 tablespoon parsley.

In a lasagna pan or a large, 9x13-inch glass casserole dish, layer ingredients in the following order: 6 noodles, ½ cottage cheese mixture, ½ mozzarella cheese, ½ meat mixture, 6 noodles, remainder of cottage cheese mixture, remainder of meat mixture, remainder of mozzarella.

Cover with foil and bake for 1 hour. Uncover lasagna, reduce oven temperature to 325°F, and bake for an additional 30 minutes.

Zucchini Lasagna

This pastaless lasagna won't weigh you down like other versions. It's perfect for a midsummer meal when your garden is cranking out the squash (use those monster zukes) and the temperature beckons you to dine alfresco.

SERVES 8 TO 10

3 large zucchini, cleaned and cut lengthwise in long strips

Water

1 teaspoon salt

4 cups marinara sauce

1 cup bread crumbs

2 pounds ricotta cheese

4 eggs, beaten lightly

4 tablespoons chopped fresh parsley

1 teaspoon dried oregano

1 teaspoon dried basil

Salt and pepper

1 cup grated Parmesan cheese

1 pound grated mozzarella cheese

Heat oven to 350°F.

Place the zucchini in a large saucepan with 1 inch of water and 1 teaspoon salt. Bring to a boil and cook until limp, about 5 minutes. Drain on paper towels.

In a 9x13-inch glass baking pan or lasagna pan, spread part of the marinara sauce in the bottom of the pan. Add ¼ cup bread crumbs, then a layer of the drained zucchini slices placed side by side to completely cover the sauce layer.

In a large bowl, combine ricotta, eggs, parsley, oregano, basil, salt and pepper to taste, half of the Parmesan cheese, and half of the remaining bread crumbs. Spoon half of this mixture on top of the zucchini. Sprinkle with half of the shredded mozzarella cheese.

Repeat layers. Cover with most of the remaining marinara sauce. Arrange remaining zucchini on top. Drizzle with the rest of the marinara sauce and the rest of the mozzarella cheese. Combine the remaining bread crumbs and Parmesan cheese, and sprinkle on top of the casserole.

Bake for 1 hour, until the top is nicely browned. Let stand for 20 minutes before serving.

Mom, is dinner ready?

While raising my four children, I was constantly being interrupted by them while trying to cook and bake. My family soon learned instead of hearing a dinner bell, they would hear the smoke alarm, and then they knew dinner was ready.

Sheila Kearney
Holton, Kansas

Mexican Lasagna

This Mexican-inspired casserole uses corn tortillas in place of pasta for a corny twist on the classic Italian dish. You'll love the flavor combinations.

SERVES 6

2 tablespoons olive oil, divided

1¼ pounds ground chicken turkey or turkey

½ cup chopped onion

1 can (4 ounces) mild chopped green chilies

Salt and black pepper

1 can (14 ounces) enchilada sauce

12 6-inch corn tortillas

2 cups shredded Mexican cheese

Sour cream for garnish

Chopped fresh cilantro for garnish

Heat oven to 350°F. Lightly grease a 9x9-inch baking dish and set aside.

In a large skillet over medium-high heat, heat 1½ tablespoons of oil. Add ground meat, onion, and green chilies; season with salt and pepper. Sauté for 10 minutes, until meat is no longer pink, breaking it into crumbles as it cooks.

Spoon a thin layer of enchilada sauce into the bottom of the prepared dish. Add a layer of four overlapping tortillas. Spoon ⅓ of the meat mixture over the tortillas. Drizzle with enchilada sauce and sprinkle with ½ cup cheese. Continue to layer in this manner until all ingredients are used, ending with a layer of cheese.

MEXICAN LASAGNA

DesmondLWF/Fotolia

Bake for 15 to 20 minutes, until hot and bubbly. Allow to cool for 10 minutes before cutting. If desired, top each serving with sour cream and cilantro.

Spinach Lasagna

This dish, a favorite of vegetarians, is just as savory and filling as its meatier cousins. Note that you'll need to start this dish the night before, as you'll get best results when it has been allowed to set overnight in the refrigerator.

SERVES 6 TO 8

1 pound ricotta cheese

2 cups shredded mozzarella cheese, divided

1 egg

1 package (10 ounces) frozen chopped spinach, thawed and drained

1 teaspoon oregano

2 cloves garlic, minced

½ teaspoon salt

Pinch of pepper

1 zucchini, thinly sliced

1 carrot, shredded

32 ounces marinara sauce, divided

12 lasagna noodles, uncooked (or enough to fill pan in layers)

1 cup water

SPINACH LASAGNA

istockphoto.com/lvinst

Grease a 9x13x3-inch baking pan and set aside.

In a large bowl, mix ricotta, 1 cup mozzarella, egg, spinach, oregano, garlic, salt, and pepper.

In a separate bowl, combine zucchini, carrot, and 1 cup of sauce. In the prepared pan, layer 1 cup of sauce, 3 noodles, and half of the ricotta cheese mixture. Add 3 more noodles and zucchini mixture. Continue with 3 more noodles and remaining ricotta cheese mixture.

Top with remaining noodles and sauce. Sprinkle with remaining 1 cup mozzarella cheese. Pour the water around the edges of the pan. Cover tightly with foil and refrigerate overnight.

To prepare, heat oven to 350°F. Bake covered for 60 to 70 minutes. Let stand for 10 to 15 minutes before serving.

Wild Rice and Turkey Casserole

This day-after-Thanksgiving dish is an easy-to-prepare family favorite. The indulgent, nutty wild rice makes a difference in this recipe, so try not to substitute with blander white or brown rice if possible.

SERVES 8

WILD RICE AND TURKEY CASSEROLE
Credit: istockphoto.com/martinturzak

1 cup wild rice

6 tablespoons butter, divided

1 cup diced fresh mushrooms

1 medium onion, chopped

2 teaspoons salt

¼ teaspoon black pepper

3 cups cooked turkey, diced

¼ cup sliced almonds

3 cups turkey or chicken broth

1½ cups heavy cream

3 tablespoons Parmesan cheese

Heat oven to 350°F. Grease a 2-quart casserole dish and set aside.

Rinse rice thoroughly in a colander and transfer to a 2-quart saucepan. Cover with boiling water and let stand for 1 hour. Drain.

In a small skillet, heat 1 tablespoon of butter and sauté mushrooms and onions until softened, about 10 minutes.

In the prepared casserole dish, combine rice, sautéed vegetables, salt, pepper, turkey, and almonds. Add broth and cream. Mix lightly.

Cover and bake for 1½ hours. Remove cover; sprinkle with cheese and dot with remaining 5 tablespoons of butter. Increase oven temperature to 450°F; bake for an additional 5 minutes.

Turkey Tetrazzini

Tetrazzini—whether turkey, chicken, tuna, or otherwise—is loved by all, but where does the name come from? The dish is named after the early twentieth-century opera star Luisa Tetrazzini, and it's believed to have been invented by a chef at the Palace Hotel in San Francisco, where Tetrazzini was a longtime resident. Recipes vary, but they usually contain some combination of meat, pasta, vegetables, almonds, and a butter-cream sauce.

SERVES 8 TO 10

8 ounces small pasta (such as penne or spiral)

4 tablespoons butter

2 teaspoons salt

6 tablespoons unbleached all-purpose flour

½ teaspoon black pepper

½ teaspoon celery salt

2 cups chicken stock

½ cup dry sherry (optional)

1 can (6 ounces) mushrooms, sliced

1 can (10½ ounces) cream of mushroom soup

½ cup slivered, toasted almonds

3 cups cubed cooked turkey or chicken

1 cup grated mozzarella cheese

3 tablespoons minced fresh parsley

TURKEY TETRAZZINI

istockphoto.com/ Lauri Patterson

Cook pasta according to package directions; drain.

Heat oven to 350°F. Grease a 2-quart casserole dish and set aside.

In a small saucepan, melt the butter over low heat. Add salt and flour; blend. Add pepper, celery salt, and stock. Cook until thickened. Add sherry, mushrooms, soup, and almonds. Mix well and heat through.

In the prepared casserole dish, alternate layers of pasta, turkey, and sauce. Top with cheese and parsley.

Bake uncovered for 45 minutes, until bubbling and golden.

Chapter 6
Main Dishes

THE MAIN DISH SERVES as the centerpiece of the meal. The oohs and aahs echo through the house as the roasted turkey atop a platter is set on the dining table at Thanksgiving. A beautifully carved, rare roast beef or beef tenderloin is served on the joyful occasion of Christmas or New Year's Day. The main dish requires some effort, but that effort won't go unnoticed.

Whether it's a grand roasted bird, a honey-baked ham, a savory pie, or a perfect fried chicken, the main dish is what sticks to your ribs. Protein and fat satisfy a hungry body. In the lean times of the olden days, these nutrients weren't always a given, but reserved for Sundays or special occasions. Cherish these recipes and take a moment to think back to your childhood. Which one do you recall most fondly?

From chicken and dumplings to meatloaf and pot roast, these comforting old-style main dishes will remind you of good times. Unfold your napkin, say a blessing, and dig in.

Beef Tenderloin with Roasted Potatoes

The choicest tenderloins come from steers or heifers. This muscle sits beneath the ribs, next to the backbone; it does very little work, and as a result is the tenderest part of the beef. Tenderloins off any animal are usually reserved for special occasions.

SERVES 8

Seasoning:

¼ cup chopped fresh parsley

2 tablespoons Dijon-style mustard

1 tablespoon cracked black pepper

Roast:

1 beef tenderloin roast
(3 to 4 pounds), well-trimmed

2 pounds small new red potatoes

4 small onions, cut lengthwise into quarters

1 tablespoon olive oil

½ teaspoon salt

⅛ teaspoon pepper

Creamy Horseradish Sauce:

½ cup mayonnaise

½ cup dairy sour cream

3 tablespoons milk

¼ cup prepared horseradish

2 tablespoons thinly sliced green onions

Preheat oven to 425°F.

Combine seasoning ingredients and spread evenly onto the surface of the roast. Place the roast on a rack in a shallow roasting pan. Insert a meat thermometer so the tip is centered in the thickest part (not resting in fat). Do not add water or cover.

In a large bowl, combine potatoes, onions, and oil; season with salt and pepper. Toss to coat evenly. Arrange the vegetables on the rack around the roast.

Roast the beef and vegetables for 55 to 65 minutes, until roast is medium-rare to medium doneness and vegetables are almost tender. Turn vegetables halfway through cooking time. Roast should reach 140°F for medium-rare, 155°F for medium. Once the desired temperature is reached, remove roast from the oven and let it stand 15 minutes before carving. (The temperature will rise about 5 degrees as it stands.) Return vegetables to the oven for 8 to 10 minutes, until tender. Carve the roast into ¼-inch slices; serve with roasted vegetables and Creamy Horseradish Sauce.

Creamy Horseradish Sauce: In a small bowl, combine mayonnaise with sour cream, milk, horseradish, and green onions; mix well to blend. Cover and refrigerate until serving. Makes 1½ cups.

Roast Beef with Blackberry Ketchup

We crave roast beef for its old-fashioned charm. It's a dish that everyone knows and loves, but no one knows how to make anymore. The flavors of anise, star anise, cinnamon, cloves, and ginger coat the roast. If you put forth the effort to make the accompanying blackberry ketchup, you won't be disappointed. This ketchup is a delicious flavor note to roast beef—perfect in summer when the blackberries are in season. This dish is a truly comforting melange of flavors to delight your senses.

SERVES 8

ROAST BEEF WITH
BLACKBERRY KETCHUP
iStockphoto.com/loooby

Roast:

1 tablespoon Chinese 5-spice seasoning

2 tablespoons sesame oil

4 pounds sirloin tip beef roast

Blackberry Ketchup:

2 cups blackberries, fresh or frozen

½ cup cider vinegar

½ cup water

¾ cup firmly packed, dark brown sugar

½ teaspoon ground cloves

½ teaspoon ground ginger

1 teaspoon ground cinnamon

¼ teaspoon cayenne pepper

½ teaspoon salt

2 tablespoons unsalted butter

Grated rind of 1 tangerine

To make roast: heat oven to 325°F.

In a small bowl, combine the 5-spice seasoning with sesame oil. Whisk until smooth. Rub the roast with the seasoning mixture.

On a rack in a shallow roasting pan, place the beef fat side up. Insert a meat thermometer into the thickest part of the beef (not touching bone or resting in fat). Do not add water or cover.

Roast to 5 degrees below desired degree of doneness, planning about 21 to 30 minutes per pound. For rare, roast to 140°F; for medium, 160°F. After desired temperature is reached, remove the roast from the oven and tent with foil. Let it stand for 15 to 20 minutes before carving. (Temperature will rise 5 degrees as the roast stands.)

Serve with blackberry ketchup, if desired.

To make blackberry ketchup: in a saucepan, combine berries, vinegar, and water. Bring to a boil; lower heat and simmer for 5 minutes.

Place a bowl under a fine mesh sieve and pour berry mixture into it, removing seeds. Return the mixture to the saucepan and add brown sugar, cloves, ginger, cinnamon, cayenne pepper, salt, butter, and grated rind. Simmer for another 10 minutes, or until the mixture is thickened. Let cool before serving.

Yankee Pot Roast

Tougher cuts of meat, such as chuck roast and 7-bone pot roast, are popular for pot roasting because they become tender and flavorful when braised slowly. This traditional pot roast is what you remember eating at Grandma's house on Sundays.

SERVES 4 TO 6

1 clove garlic, crushed

1 teaspoon dried oregano leaves, crushed

½ teaspoon lemon-pepper seasoning

½ teaspoon salt

1 boneless beef arm pot roast (3 to 3½ pounds)

1 tablespoon olive oil

¾ cup plus 1 tablespoon water

8 small new red potatoes, halved

2 medium carrots, peeled and cut into 2½-inch pieces

2 medium parsnips, peeled and cut into pieces

1 small leek, cut into 1½-inch pieces

2 teaspoons cornstarch

YANKEE POT ROAST

iStockphoto.com/cislander

In a small bowl, combine garlic, oregano, lemon-pepper seasoning, and salt to form a paste. Rub paste evenly over the surface of the pot roast. Heat the oil in a Dutch oven over medium-high heat. Brown the roast on all sides. Pour off drippings.

Add ¾ cup water and reduce heat to low. Cover tightly and cook slowly on the stovetop for 1¾ hours. Add potatoes, carrots, parsnips, and leek; cover and continue cooking for 30 minutes or more until vegetables and beef are tender.

Transfer the roast to a warm platter. Strain the cooking liquid, reserving 1 cup; skim and discard fat. Dissolve cornstarch in remaining 1 tablespoon of water; stir into the cooking liquid. Bring to a boil. Cook for 1 minute, until thickened, stirring constantly.

Trim excess fat from the roast before serving. Serve with vegetables and gravy.

Irish Honey Pot Roast

The honey and ale (or cider), plus the carrots, parsnips, and leeks, combine for unique flavors we'd expect from an Irish farm supper. Simple and wholesome, this dish will be loved by all.

SERVES 8 TO 10

½ cup unbleached all-purpose flour

1 teaspoon salt

1 teaspoon pepper

4- to 5-pound pot roast, 7-blade, rump or top round

2 tablespoons olive oil

14 ounces beef broth

½ cup honey

1 cup Irish ale or apple cider

4 cloves garlic, minced

2 teaspoons dried thyme

2 cups chopped carrots

2 cups chopped potatoes

2 cups chopped parsnips

2 cups chopped leeks

½ cup cold water

Heat oven to 375°F.

In a medium bowl, combine flour, salt, and pepper. Dredge the roast in the flour mixture, coating all sides. Reserve remaining flour mixture.

In a large Dutch oven, heat the oil over medium-high heat. Add the roast and sear on all sides. Then sear and brown the top and bottom of the roast, about 4 to 5 minutes each. Add broth, honey, ale, garlic, and thyme. Cover and roast in the oven for 1½ hours.

Add the vegetables. Cover and cook for an additional hour, or until meat is fork tender. Remove the meat and vegetables to a platter. Tent loosely with foil to keep warm.

Add cold water to the reserved flour mixture; whisk into the juices in the Dutch oven. Place the Dutch oven over medium-high heat and bring mixture to a boil. Continue to cook, stirring constantly, until gravy is thickened. Season to taste with additional salt and pepper. Serve with meat and vegetables.

If desired, you may cook the roast in a slow cooker. Follow directions above through browning of the pot roast. Place the vegetables in the bottom of the slow cooker and place the meat on top, cutting as necessary to fit. Add the remaining ingredients, except water. Cover and cook on Low for 8 to 10 hours. Prepare gravy as directed above.

Slow Cooker After-Work Beef Pot Roast

When you crave the comfort of a pot roast, but don't have time to stand around the kitchen babying one, utilize this slow-cooked version.

SERVES 8

1 envelope (0.7 ounce) Italian dressing mix

1 boneless beef chuck shoulder pot roast or bottom round rump roast (3 to 3½ pounds)

2 large onions, cut into 8 wedges

2 garlic cloves, peeled

2 red bell peppers, cut into 1½-inch pieces

½ cup beef broth

2 zucchini, cut into ¼-inch slices

2½ tablespoons cornstarch, dissolved in 2 tablespoons water

Salt and pepper

Press the dressing mix evenly onto all surfaces of the roast. In a 4½- to 5½-quart slow cooker, place the onions and garlic; top with the roast. Add the bell peppers and broth. Cover and cook on high for 5 hours or on low for 8 hours. Add zucchini. Continue cooking, covered, 30 minutes, until pot roast is fork tender.

Remove the pot roast and vegetables. Strain and reserve the cooking liquid; skim off the fat. In a medium saucepan, combine 2 cups of the cooking liquid and the cornstarch mixture. Bring to a boil, stirring constantly; cook and stir 1 minute, until thickened.

Carve pot roast into slices; season with salt and pepper. Serve with vegetables and gravy.

Yearning for steak

Looking back as a grownup, I kick myself a little bit thinking back to the lack of love my brothers and I showed for my mom's pot roast. I love roast, just had slow cooker roast with cabbage, carrots, and potatoes for dinner last night and lunch today. But as kids growing up around a cattle farm, I would give my big toe to go back in time and eat steaks as often as we did growing up. To us, a real treat was what we'd request on our birthdays—homemade pizza, campfire hotdogs with baked beans, tacos (my mom did fry corn tortillas, which made the meal)—and it'd never be steaks. My, how times have changed—give me a ribeye any day of the week.

Caleb D. Regan
Lawrence, Kansas

Chicken and Dumplings

At the top of our comfort foods list is this dish. Nothing beats homemade, slow-cooked chicken and dumplings when you're under the weather or in a celebratory mood.

SERVES 6

3 cups unbleached all-purpose flour

¼ teaspoon baking soda

¼ teaspoon salt

2 tablespoons pure lard or butter

1 cup ice water

1 whole chicken, cut into pieces (about 4 pounds)

1 tablespoon seasoning salt

3½ quarts water

½ small onion, chopped very fine

1 stalk celery, chopped very fine

1 carrot, chopped very fine

¼ cup butter

Salt and pepper

1 teaspoon poultry seasoning

CHICKEN AND DUMPLINGS

iStockphoto.com/eurobanks

In a large bowl, sift flour, baking soda, and salt. Cut in the lard until mixture resembles coarse crumbs. Stir in ice water until mixture forms a ball. Divide dough in half and shape each into a ball. Wrap in plastic wrap and refrigerate for at least 2 hours, or overnight.

Remove skin from chicken breasts, thighs, and back; leave skin on legs and wings. Season chicken pieces with seasoning salt and place in a large stockpot. Add water, onion, celery, carrot, and butter. Bring to a boil; reduce heat to simmer. Cook for about 1½ hours, or until chicken falls off the bone. Remove chicken and strip the meat from the bones. Return chicken meat to the pot.

Remove one dough ball from refrigerator. Pull off pieces of dough and roll into rough balls. Drop into the simmering broth and simmer for about 15 minutes, or until dumplings are cooked through. Add more water if necessary. Season broth with salt, pepper, and poultry seasoning while dumplings are cooking. Use the second dough ball to make a second batch of dumplings, or freeze it for later use.

Henrietta's Spicy Fried Chicken

When Memphis-born Henrietta relocated to Lincoln County, Kansas, to be with her husband after World War II, she found herself smack-dab in the middle of bland—bland food, that is. So she took her mother-in-law's fried chicken recipe and gave it some zing to create this spicier version. Serve with your favorite potato salad and coleslaw for the perfect summertime picnic.

SERVES 4 TO 6

1 to 2 teaspoons black pepper

½ teaspoon poultry seasoning

½ teaspoon paprika

½ teaspoon cayenne

¼ teaspoon dry mustard

1 frying chicken (2½ to 3½ pounds), cut up into 8 pieces

¼ cup all-purpose unbleached flour

2¼ teaspoons garlic salt

¼ to ½ teaspoon salt

¼ teaspoon celery salt

Lard for frying

In a large bowl, combine the black pepper, poultry seasoning, paprika, cayenne, and mustard. Dredge the chicken pieces in the spices.

In a paper or plastic bag, combine the flour, garlic salt, salt, and celery salt; shake to mix. Add chicken, a few pieces at a time, and shake to coat.

Heat the lard to 340°F and 2 inches deep in an electric skillet, or on medium heat in large cast-iron skillet. Add the chicken pieces and fry for 30 minutes, turning every 10 minutes.

Increase the heat to 355°F for an electric skillet, or medium-high for a regular skillet. Fry for an additional 5 minutes, or until the meat is no longer pink at the bone. Remove the chicken from the fat and drain on paper towels.

Chicken and noodles, the ultimate comfort food

It wouldn't be Christmas without my Aunt Sherry's homemade chicken and noodles. She wakes up at 3:00 a.m. Christmas morning to cook the chicken and make the noodles from scratch. (She learned how to make this recipe from my great aunt, so it's been a family favorite for decades.)

I'm not a comfort food fanatic, but I could care less what else is served that day. Thankfully, Sherry makes enough for us all to have leftovers, which I promptly hide from my husband once we return home.

Brandy Ernzen
Lawrence, Kansas

Southern Fried Chicken

Born in the South, this native recipe embodies southern hospitality and Sunday suppers after church. The key ingredient is buttermilk, which, along with other dairy products like yogurt, tenderizes meat. The result is a crispier, juicier piece of fried chicken.

SERVES 4 TO 6

1 cup all-purpose unbleached flour

½ teaspoon salt

½ teaspoon white pepper

2 cups buttermilk

1 frying chicken (2 to 2½ pounds), cut up into 8 pieces

Lard for frying

Combine the flour, salt, and pepper in a paper bag. Place the buttermilk in a large bowl. Set both aside.

In a heavy cast-iron skillet, heat the lard to 340°F and 1½ to 2 inches deep (start with 2 cups, adding more as needed). One by one, coat the chicken pieces in buttermilk, then shake in the bag until coated with seasoned flour.

Add the chicken pieces to the hot fat, leaving a little space between the pieces so they're not crowded. Reduce the heat to medium and cook until the underside is golden brown, about 15 minutes. Turn and cook until the other side is brown. Reduce the heat to low; cover and cook an additional 10 minutes, or until chicken is no longer pink at the bone. Remove the chicken from the fat and drain on paper towels.

Oven-Fried Honey Chicken

We love oven-fried chicken for its simplicity—no messy oil to clean up afterward. The honey and vinegar give this chicken a sweet-and-sour flavor, and the bread crumbs deliver the crunch we crave in fried chicken.

SERVES 6

¼ cup honey

2 tablespoons balsamic vinegar or red wine vinegar

1½ cups dried bread crumbs

1 tablespoon olive oil

6 boneless, skinless chicken breast halves (about 2 pounds)

Heat oven to 375°F.

In a medium bowl, whisk together honey and vinegar. Pour bread crumbs into a separate bowl. Set both bowls aside.

Line a baking pan (large enough to hold all chicken pieces in one layer) with foil. Spread oil over the foil.

Roll chicken pieces in honey mixture, then in bread crumbs. Place in pan. Bake for 30 minutes, or until cooked through.

SOUTHERN FRIED
CHICKEN

Monkey Business/Fotolia

Southwestern Oven-Fried Chicken

Cornmeal delivers even more of that crunch we love in oven-fried chicken. This combination of spices can't be beat. Serve with cilantro-perfumed rice and salsa.

SERVES 4

SOUTHWESTERN OVEN-FRIED CHICKEN

iStockphoto.com/robeo

3 slices white bread, torn into small pieces

3 tablespoons fresh cilantro leaves

2 tablespoons yellow cornmeal

2 tablespoons pine nuts

2 large cloves garlic, peeled

1½ teaspoons ground cumin

½ teaspoon crumbled oregano leaves

½ teaspoon salt, divided

¼ teaspoon cayenne pepper

⅛ teaspoon ground cloves

2 teaspoons egg white

2 tablespoons Dijon mustard

1 tablespoon water

2 teaspoons honey

4 broiler-fryer chicken drumsticks, skinned

4 broiler-fryer chicken thighs, skinned

¼ teaspoon pepper

Heat oven to 400°F. Grease a jellyroll pan and set aside.

In a food processor container or blender, place bread, cilantro, cornmeal, pine nuts, garlic, cumin, oregano, ¼ teaspoon salt, cayenne pepper, and ground cloves; process to form fine crumbs. Add egg white and mix until moist. Place mixture on a large, shallow plate; set aside.

In a small bowl, mix together the mustard, water, and honey; brush evenly over chicken pieces; sprinkle with pepper and remaining salt. Dip chicken, one piece at a time, in cornmeal mixture and press gently to adhere a thin coating.

Place chicken on a rack in the prepared pan and bake for about 40 minutes, or until chicken is crisp and brown, and fork can be inserted with ease. Serve immediately.

Herbed Ham with Savory Gravy

This mustardy, crusty baked ham is a real treat. It's not the usual sweet preparation for a ham, but once you make it, you'll always come back to this recipe.

SERVES 8

1 ham, boneless (pork leg), 6 to 8 pounds, tied (not netted)

¾ cup Dijon mustard, divided

1 cup dry bread crumbs

6 tablespoons fresh chopped parsley, divided

3 tablespoons olive oil

2 tablespoons fresh chopped rosemary, or 2 tablespoons dried rosemary, crushed

1 teaspoon salt

¼ teaspoon ground pepper

2 cups water

1½ cups red wine

Preheat oven to 350°F.

Trim excess fat from ham; spread ½ cup mustard evenly over the ham.

In a bowl, mix bread crumbs, 4 tablespoons parsley, olive oil, rosemary, salt, and pepper. Press crumb mixture evenly over ham. Place ham in a roasting pan. Add 2 cups water to the pan; tent with foil.

Roast 1½ hours; remove foil. Roast 1½ hours more or until meat thermometer registers 155°F internal temperature, adding water to roasting pan as needed.

Remove ham from the pan; let rest, loosely covered, 10 to 15 minutes.

While ham is resting, drain pan drippings into a measuring cup, pouring off any excess fat. To the roasting pan, add wine and drippings. Set over two burners, if necessary, and bring to a boil over medium heat, stirring to loosen browned bits from the pan. Reduce heat to low; simmer 10 minutes. Thicken gravy with flour, if desired. Stir in remaining mustard and parsley; heat through. Serve ham with gravy.

Helping Grandma with homemade noodles

I remember as a little girl helping Grandma make homemade noodles for chicken and noodles.

She would put me in the chair, and I would get on my knees so that I could dip my hands in the flour and spread it on the table so she could roll out the dough. I was always amazed at how she would cut the strips of noodles with a knife and they would be so straight. I know the reason they always tasted so good was because Grandma's hands made them.

Anita Fisher
Topeka, Kansas

Ham with Honey Crust

Ham with a sweet, sticky crust is a comfort-food favorite. This recipe uses wholesome honey in place of the usual cola. Serve this next Easter and enjoy sandwiches with the leftovers.

SERVES 10 TO 12

1 uncooked ham, 6 to 8 pounds, washed

1 tablespoon plus 1 teaspoon whole cloves, divided

½ teaspoon black peppercorns

1 teaspoon dry mustard

½ cup celery leaves

½ cup vinegar, divided

1 cup honey, divided

2 eggs

1½ cups water

½ cup chopped, seedless raisins

Place ham in a large Dutch oven with warm water completely covering it. Add 1 tablespoon cloves, peppercorns, mustard, celery leaves, ¼ cup vinegar, and ¼ cup honey. Cook slowly, covered, over medium-low heat, allowing 25 minutes per pound. Let ham cool in water; remove skin.

Heat oven to 400°F.

Score the ham with a sharp knife in a diagonal pattern. Repeat scoring, diagonally in the opposite direction, to create a crisscross pattern. Insert whole cloves into the meat at the crossings.

Combine eggs and ¼ cup honey; brush over the surface of the ham. Bake for 45 minutes, until golden brown, basting several times with the drippings.

Combine remaining ¼ cup vinegar, water, remaining ½ cup honey, and raisins in a saucepan. Bring to a boil; reduce heat and simmer until thickened, like a syrup. Serve hot with sliced ham.

ROAST HERBED LEG OF LAMB WITH NEW POTATOES

Karen K. Will

Roast Herbed Leg of Lamb with New Potatoes

Grass-fed lamb doesn't taste anything like the lamb you've had from the grocery meat counter. It's mild and tender with an ideal amount of marbling, and it's best served medium-rare, so don't overcook it.

SERVES 6 TO 8

6 cloves garlic, peeled, divided

1 teaspoon sea salt

½ teaspoon freshly ground pepper

3 tablespoons olive oil, divided

1 tablespoon Dijon mustard

½ cup fresh mint

2½ pounds grass-fed leg of lamb

2 pounds new potatoes, scrubbed and left unpeeled

Place 3 cloves of garlic, salt, pepper, 1 tablespoon olive oil, mustard, and mint in a food processor and process until a coarse-textured paste forms.

Rub the paste over the lamb, coating well, and let stand at room temperature for at least 30 minutes.

Heat oven to 450°F.

Place potatoes, remaining 2 tablespoons olive oil, remaining 3 cloves garlic (whole and peeled), and an additional pinch of salt and pepper in medium bowl; toss well.

Put the potatoes in the bottom of a large roasting pan. Place lamb on top of the potatoes. Position a rack in the lower third of the oven. Roast lamb and potatoes for 1 to 1½ hours, until a meat thermometer registers 140°F (medium-rare).

Remove lamb from the oven, place meat on a plate, and tent with foil. Allow to rest for 15 to 20 minutes.

Arrange potatoes and lamb on a platter. Garnish with additional fresh mint and serve.

Horseradish Meatloaf

Horseradish definitely kicks meatloaf up a notch in flavor. Add more or less than the recipe calls for, according to your taste. Leftover meatloaf makes great sandwich fixings, and since this recipe calls for a dry top, it lends itself particularly well to this purpose.

SERVES 6

2 pounds ground beef

1 large onion, chopped

½ cup old-fashioned oatmeal

½ cup Italian bread crumbs

2 to 4 teaspoons prepared horseradish

2 to 4 cloves garlic, crushed, or 2 to 4 teaspoons minced garlic

1 teaspoon black pepper

4 to 6 eggs

Heat oven to 350°F.

Combine all ingredients in a large bowl, adding enough eggs for moist consistency, using your hands to blend well. Place in large, flat pan or dish and pat into a shape to fit, leaving 1 inch of space around the meatloaf.

Add 1 inch of water to the pan, cover with foil, and bake 1½ to 2 hours (depending on preferred doneness).

Uncover meatloaf 30 minutes before removing from oven to brown the top. Place meatloaf on a platter and slice to serve.

HORSERADISH MEATLOAF

azurite/Fotolia

Meatloaf Supreme

This deliciously moist, glazed meatloaf combines a variety of flavors. The bell pepper and onion keep it from drying out, and when minced finely in a food processor, these ingredients blend well into the meat. The spices and sweet sauce deliver a memorable finish.

SERVES 6

1 small onion

½ green bell pepper

½ cup milk

1 egg

¾ cup seasoned bread crumbs

1 teaspoon dried basil

1 tablespoon dried parsley

⅛ teaspoon black pepper

1½ pounds ground beef

3 tablespoons ketchup

1 tablespoon honey

½ teaspoon Worcestershire sauce

MEATLOAF SUPREME

MSPhotographic/Fotolia

Heat oven to 350°F. Line a 9x5-inch loaf pan with foil, spray with cooking spray, and set aside.

Mince onion and bell pepper, using a food processor if available.

In a large bowl, combine milk and egg. Add bread crumbs, basil, parsley, and black pepper. Stir until blended. Add onion and bell pepper; mix well. Add beef and mix, using clean hands, to combine ingredients. Place mixture in a loaf pan and gently shape; do not pack.

In a small bowl, combine ketchup, honey, and Worcestershire sauce; blend well. Spread evenly over top of meatloaf.

Bake until cooked through, about 1 hour. Place pan on a wire rack and let stand for 5 minutes. Remove foil and lift meatloaf out of pan and place on a serving platter. Slice and serve.

Bob's Meatloaf

Bob is one of our readers, and he is a meatloaf aficionado. This is his award-winning recipe, and his advice is to "keep in mind that meatloaf doesn't always have to be 100 percent beef. Try mixing ground meats like pork, lamb, turkey, and venison into the beef for variety."

SERVES 6

4 slices white bread, cut into cubes

½ cup milk

3 eggs, lightly beaten

1 tablespoon Worcestershire sauce

2 tablespoons plus ½ cup ketchup, divided

3 tablespoons prepared mustard, divided

¼ cup finely chopped onion

¼ cup finely chopped celery

1 teaspoon lemon juice

1 clove garlic, minced

2 pounds ground beef

1 tablespoon brown sugar

BOB'S MEATLOAF

dreambigphotos/Fotolia

Heat oven to 350°F.

Place bread cubes in a large mixing bowl; add milk and let stand until milk is absorbed. Add eggs, Worcestershire sauce, 2 tablespoons ketchup, 1 tablespoon mustard, onion, celery, lemon juice, garlic, and ground beef; mix well. Shape into 2 loaves and place in a large, shallow baking pan. Bake for about 30 minutes.

Combine remaining ½ cup ketchup, remaining 2 tablespoons mustard, and brown sugar; blend well and spread over the baked loaves. Return to the oven and bake for an additional 30 minutes.

Shepherd's Pie

Sometimes known as cottage pie in early cookbooks, this dish was a means of using leftover roasted meat of any kind. Lamb, mutton, or beef can all be used. For the best flavor and nutrition, procure grass-fed meat when possible.

SERVES 6 TO 8

SHEPHERD'S PIE

Karen K. Will

1½ pounds Yukon Gold potatoes, unpeeled

2 tablespoons olive oil

2 pounds ground grass-fed lamb

1 tablespoon dried rosemary

1 tablespoon dried thyme

4 cloves garlic, minced

Salt and pepper

1 large carrot, peeled and grated

1 large onion, grated

1 teaspoon Worcestershire sauce

1 can (6 ounces) tomato paste

¼ cup red wine

¼ cup chicken stock

¼ cup heavy cream

3 tablespoons butter

1 egg yolk

¼ cup finely grated Parmesan cheese

Heat oven to 400°F.

Scrub potatoes clean and place in a large pot of salted water. Boil for about 20 minutes, until easily pierced with fork.

Meanwhile, in a large, deep skillet, heat olive oil for 1 minute. Add lamb and stir, breaking into a fine mince. Stir in rosemary, thyme, garlic, and season with salt and pepper. Add carrot and onion and stir until everything is well incorporated.

Stir in Worcestershire sauce and tomato paste. Add red wine and let simmer for 1 minute. Stir in chicken stock and cook for another minute. Turn off heat and set skillet aside.

When potatoes are done, drain and return to the pan. Add cream, butter, and egg yolk, and season with salt and pepper. Mash mixture together, skins and all; set aside.

Spoon meat mixture into a deep casserole dish (or if you used an ovenproof skillet, just smooth down meat mixture), then carefully spread mashed potato mixture on top using the back of a large spoon. Sprinkle on Parmesan cheese. Drag a fork over the top of the potatoes to create peaks and valleys.

Bake, uncovered, for 20 minutes, until top is nicely browned. Broil for 1 minute, if desired, for a little more browning. Allow to cool for a few minutes before serving.

Chicken Pot Pie

Oh, the comfort of a chicken pot pie—or any pot pie, for that matter. It's the perfect vehicle for a store-bought rotisserie chicken or last night's leftovers. A pot pie is surprisingly easy, too, and can be whipped up in a jiffy. Substitute ¼ cup nut meal (hazelnut, almond) for an equal amount of flour in the crust for a delightful flavor twist.

SERVES 8

CHICKEN POT PIE
Karen K. Will

Crust:

1½ cups all-purpose unbleached flour

½ teaspoon salt

½ cup butter (1 stick) or pure lard, or a combination

5 tablespoons ice water, divided

Filling:

2 tablespoons butter

1 cup chopped onion

1 cup sliced celery or fennel

1 cup chopped carrots

¼ cup all-purpose unbleached flour

1 teaspoon poultry seasoning

½ teaspoon salt

½ teaspoon pepper

1 cup chicken broth

¾ cup whole milk or half-and-half

2½ cups cooked, chopped chicken

1 cup frozen peas

¼ cup fresh parsley

To make the crust: Stir together the flour and salt in medium bowl. Using a pastry blender, cut in the butter until mixture resembles coarse meal. Sprinkle 1 tablespoon ice water over the mixture and toss with fork. Sprinkle additional water, 1 tablespoon at a time, over mixture until it's moistened and comes together in a ball. Refrigerate pastry until filling is ready.

Heat oven to 400°F. Butter a 2-quart casserole dish or 8x8x2-inch baking dish and set aside.

To make the filling: In a saucepan over medium-low heat, melt the butter. Add onion, celery, and carrots, and sauté for 5 to 7 minutes, until tender.

Stir in the flour, poultry seasoning, salt, and pepper, and cook for 3 minutes. Whisk in the broth and milk, and cook until thick and bubbly. Stir in the chicken, peas, and parsley.

Turn the pastry dough out onto a floured surface and roll it out 1 inch larger than the dish. Pour the hot filling into the prepared baking dish and place the pastry on top. Use a fork to crimp the edges, flute with your fingers, or just trim edges for a rustic-style crust. Use a sharp knife to cut slits in the crust to allow steam to escape.

Bake for 30 to 35 minutes, until golden brown and bubbling. Let cool for 20 minutes before serving.

Autumn Chicken Pot Pie

This special pie combines the classic fall flavors of apples and cranberries with the savory standbys of chicken, onions, and carrots. Topped with a crust flavored with ginger and lemon zest, this pie is the perfect dish for a potluck or harvest supper.

SERVES 6

Crust:

1 cup unbleached all-purpose flour

1 teaspoon ground ginger

1 teaspoon grated lemon zest

½ teaspoon salt

⅓ cup butter, softened

3 tablespoons cold water

Filling:

1 cup pearl onions

2 medium carrots, cut into slices

2 tablespoons butter

¼ cup unbleached all-purpose flour

1 tablespoon minced fresh ginger

2 cups chicken broth

1 medium Granny Smith apple, peeled, cored, and cut into chunks

¼ cup dried cranberries

2 tablespoons lemon juice

2 cups cubed cooked chicken (leftover from roast chicken or freshly poached)

⅛ teaspoon salt

½ teaspoon freshly ground pepper

To make crust: In a large bowl, combine flour, ginger, lemon zest, and salt. Using a pastry blender, cut in butter until the mixture resembles coarse crumbs. Sprinkle water over the mixture and toss with a fork. The dough should be just barely moistened, enough to hold together when formed into a ball. Add more water if needed. Form dough into a flat disk and wrap in plastic. Refrigerate until needed.

Heat oven to 450°F.

To make the filling: Drop pearl onions into boiling water for 30 seconds; drain and peel. Steam pearl onions and carrots until tender.

In a large saucepan over medium heat, melt the butter. Whisk in flour and ginger until smooth. Reduce heat to low and gradually whisk in the chicken broth.

Stir in the steamed pearl onions and carrots, apples, cranberries, lemon juice, and chicken. Simmer for 5 minutes, stirring regularly. Stir in salt and pepper. Spoon filling into a deep, 10-inch ceramic or glass pie dish.

On a lightly floured surface, roll dough out into a circle, about 12 inches in diameter. Lay the dough over top of the pie dish. Trim and crimp the edges. Use a small knife to cut several slits in the center of the pie. (Alternatively, make decorative cuts in pie crust before setting it on top of pie.)

Set the pie on a baking sheet and place in the oven on the middle rack. Bake for 15 minutes. Reduce temperature to 400°F and continue baking for an additional 20 minutes, until pie bubbles around the edges and the top is nicely browned. Serve hot.

Perfect Roast Turkey

Roasting a turkey doesn't have to be intimidating. Neither does making gravy. Here is our simplified recipe for making that perfect roast bird—complete with gravy—for the holidays. Make this once, and you'll never have to glance at a recipe again.

SERVES 10 TO 12

1 turkey (10 to 12 pounds)

1 stick unsalted butter, room temperature

2 teaspoons dried rosemary

2 teaspoons dried thyme

2 teaspoons dried sage

1 teaspoon dried marjoram

1 teaspoon dried celery seed

Salt and freshly ground pepper

8 cups turkey stock or canned chicken broth, divided

PERFECT ROAST TURKEY
evgenyb/Fotolia

Place oven rack in the lowest position; heat oven to 325°F.

Rinse turkey inside and out with cold water and pat dry. Pull wing tips up and tuck between wings and body; place turkey, breast side up, on a rack in an open roasting pan. Rub turkey with softened butter.

In a small bowl, crush herbs together and rub over turkey. Season turkey with salt and pepper. Insert a meat thermometer in the thigh muscle just above and beyond the lower part of the thighbone but not touching the bone, pointing toward the body.

Tightly cover breast area with aluminum foil. Pour 2 cups stock into the bottom of roaster and roast, basting turkey all over every 30 minutes for about 2 hours (lift up the foil to reach the breast area). Remove foil to allow breast skin to brown; roast for about another hour until internal temperature reaches 180 degrees deep in the thigh. At this temperature, juices should be clear, not reddish pink, when thigh muscle is pierced deeply.

Remove from oven; loosen browned bits on the bottom of roaster and pour drippings into a 2-quart glass measuring cup. Allow turkey to rest for at least 20 minutes. Transfer to a platter and carve.

To make gravy: After drippings have settled for at least 5 minutes, skim off fat and reserve. Add enough stock or broth to drippings to make 6 cups. Add melted butter to reserved fat to make ½ cup. In a saucepan over low heat, heat the turkey fat mixture. Whisk in ½ cup all-purpose flour and cook until lightly browned. Add drippings mixture and continue whisking until thickened, about 2 minutes. Keep gravy warm until serving.

Stuffed Turkey Breast

When the number of guests doesn't call for a whole roasted turkey, opt for this scaled-down version. Stuffing the breast isn't entirely easy and does require patience, but the stuffing will be so flavorful, having absorbed the benefit of the rendered fat while roasting.

SERVES 10

1½ sticks butter, divided

¾ cup chopped onion

½ cup chopped celery

2 teaspoons poultry seasoning

½ teaspoon salt

¼ teaspoon pepper

½ cup milk

2 eggs, slightly beaten

2 cups dry cornbread stuffing mix

2 cups coarse, dry whole-wheat bread crumbs

5-pound turkey breast, thawed

Heat oven to 325°F.

Melt 1 stick of butter in a large skillet; add onion and celery. Sauté until tender, about 8 minutes. Remove from heat; stir in poultry seasoning, salt, and pepper. Add milk and eggs; mix well. Gently toss in cornbread stuffing and bread crumbs.

Loosen the skin of the turkey breast by gently pushing your hand between the skin and flesh. Leave about 1 inch of skin attached around the edge to hold the stuffing in. Place stuffing between the flesh and skin; place remaining stuffing in a buttered casserole dish and bake, uncovered, for 30 to 35 minutes.

Place the stuffed turkey breast on a rack in a roasting pan. Melt remaining butter and brush over the turkey. Bake, uncovered, for 3 to 3½ hours, basting frequently with melted butter. When the turkey reaches the desired brownness, tent the roasting pan with foil to prevent further browning. When a meat thermometer, inserted in the thickest part of the muscle, reaches 170°F, it's done; the center of the stuffing should be 165°F. Let the meat stand for 15 minutes before carving. Transfer to a serving platter and garnish with steamed miniature squash and thyme, if desired.

Smoked turkey a bit too long

Now that I am a grownup and a chef, I have had a few food misadventures of my own. A few years ago I built a homemade smoker and decided to smoke a turkey for Thanksgiving. Since it was only for two of us, I broke the turkey down and just smoked the legs. Well, being new to smoking I made the mistake of smoking the legs as long as you would smoke a whole bird. It was like eating charcoal. The only saving grace of that Thanksgiving was going to see *The Muppets* and stuffing our faces with popcorn.

J. Alexander Stewart
Chapel Hill, North Carolina

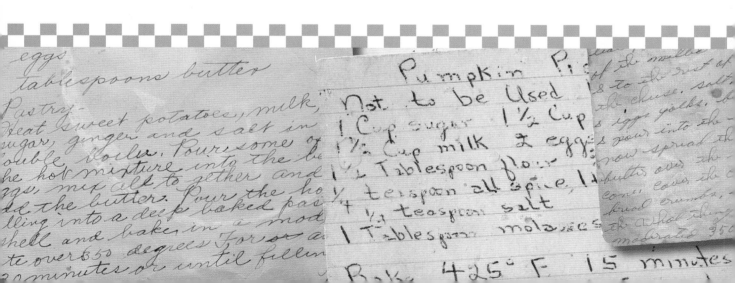

Chapter 7
Sides

SIDE DISHES ARE THE glue that hold together a meal. From the Thanksgiving smorgasbord of sides surrounding the turkey—mashed potatoes, green beans, sweet potato casserole, and dressings—to the church potluck of endless side dishes, to the modern Meatless Mondays where sides take center stage, these diverse dishes have great significance.

Meatless Mondays weren't formerly a trend, but a matter of necessity. During hard times, whether that was the Great Depression or World War II, our ancestors made do with whatever they could eke out of their garden or get cheaply from the market. Cooks readily traded new

and inventive recipes born from the absence of luxury. At *Grit* we're always looking to creatively pinch a penny, so you'll find recipes here—like scalloped eggplant, stuffed zucchini, and spiced beets—that make the most of common garden vegetables and pantry staples.

From the perfect macaroni and cheese to a mouthwatering chicken gravy, these comfort foods recall the days of Sunday suppers when nothing was on the agenda but church and cooking the big family meal.

Barbecued Baked Beans

Old-fashioned baked beans are always made with salt pork. Ask the butcher at your local supermarket or butcher shop for it; most will have it. Bacon can be substituted, but it will render a smokier flavor. If you can get slab bacon, score it and use it like salt pork, or cube it and eat it with the beans. You can soak the beans overnight in water instead of tomato juice, which will make the beans taste less acidic.

SERVES 10

2 cups dry navy or pea beans

6 cups tomato juice, divided

½ pound salt pork or bacon

½ cup packed light brown sugar

1 teaspoon dry mustard

½ teaspoon black pepper

1 tablespoon Worcestershire sauce

¾ cup onion, finely chopped

3 teaspoons salt

1 tablespoon red or cider vinegar (optional)

Rinse the beans and soak overnight in 5 cups of the tomato juice.

Transfer the beans and tomato juice to a 5-quart Dutch oven. Cover and simmer over medium heat for 1½ hours or until beans are tender. Do not boil.

Heat oven to 300°F.

Wash and score the salt pork. Cut in slashes ½ inch apart just through the rind. Press into the top of beans. In a bowl, mix the remaining 1 cup tomato juice with the brown sugar, mustard, pepper, Worcestershire sauce, and onion. Pour the mixture over the beans.

Cover and bake for 2 hours.

Remove the cover. Stir in the salt and vinegar. Lift the salt pork to the top of the beans again. Bake uncovered for 30 to 40 minutes more or until beans are brown, but not burned.

BARBECUED BAKED BEANS

iStockphoto.com/Lauri Patterson

Old-Fashioned Green Beans

These are the smoky, sweet green beans you'll get when you order them in small-town diners and roadside cafes. They're made the good old-fashioned way with the magical elixir of bacon, brown sugar, and lard.

SERVES 8

OLD-FASHIONED
GREEN BEANS
iStockphoto.com/HittProductions

1 tablespoon lard or butter

12 slices bacon, cut into ½-inch pieces

¼ cup packed dark brown sugar

1½ cups water

2 pounds fresh green beans, trimmed and broken into 2-inch pieces

Heat lard or butter in a large skillet over medium heat; add bacon and cook, stirring frequently, for 5 to 7 minutes, until browned.

Add brown sugar and water, stirring to mix well. Bring mixture to a boil. Add beans and reduce heat to low. Cover and simmer for 50 to 60 minutes, until beans are soft and all the liquid has been absorbed.

Mamaw's Baked Lima Beans

The words *lima beans* usually elicit scrunched-up noses and downturned lips, but these slow-cooked, melt-in-your-mouth, buttery soft beans with pork are a bona fide comfort food for country folks, perfect for Sunday supper. Trust us.

SERVES 4

1 cup dry baby lima beans

6 cups water

½ cup diced salt pork or bacon

½ cup thinly sliced onion

1 cup diced carrots

¼ teaspoon dry mustard

Black pepper and dried red pepper flakes

2 cups boiling water

2 tablespoons butter

Rinse the beans. Cover with the water in a large Dutch oven or heavy kettle. Over medium-high heat, bring to boiling and boil for 3 minutes.

Turn off the heat; cover the pot and let stand for about 1 hour. Drain the beans and discard the water.

Heat oven to 375°F.

In a heavy skillet, cook the salt pork or bacon over medium heat until browned. Add the onions and carrots; sauté until softened. Add the mixture to the beans and mix well. Stir in the mustard and season with peppers.

Turn the mixture into a shallow baking pan. Stir in boiling water and dot with butter. Cover and bake for about 3 hours until beans are buttery soft.

Dad's Favorite Spiced Beets

Dads always have their favorite foods, not always loved by the rest of the family. But the way to a man's heart is through his stomach, so go ahead and give him what he wants. You just might find yourself a new favorite.

SERVES 4

2½ cups cooked, skinned, and sliced beets

½ cup cider vinegar

1 onion, peeled and diced

1 tablespoon granulated sugar

¼ teaspoon peppercorns

2 small pieces stick cinnamon

½ teaspoon whole cloves

¼ teaspoon salt

Place all ingredients in a large saucepan and bring to a boil. Lower heat and simmer for about 10 minutes. Remove from heat and let stand overnight to blend flavors thoroughly.

Refrigerate for several hours before serving. Consume within 1 week.

DAD'S FAVORITE SPICED BEETS

Karen K. Will

Asparagus Supreme

A smooth and rich hollandaise sauce spooned over asparagus, Eggs Benedict, or your favorite vegetable dish works double duty. It's elegant and presents well for company, yet comforting in that you feel as though you've truly eaten something special afterward.

SERVES 4

1 tablespoon cornstarch

¼ teaspoon salt

⅛ teaspoon paprika

8 tablespoons butter, softened, divided

½ cup boiling water

1 tablespoon lemon juice

2 egg yolks, beaten

1 large bunch asparagus, cooked and drained

In a large nonreactive bowl or top of a double boiler, mix together cornstarch, salt, paprika, and 2 tablespoons butter. Add the boiling water and cook atop a double boiler with just-simmering water until thickened.

Add lemon juice and egg yolks. Cook, stirring constantly, until smooth and thick. Add the remaining 6 tablespoons butter and beat until smooth. Place hot asparagus on a serving platter and spoon sauce over all.

ASPARAGUS SUPREME

Kati Molin/Fotolia

Warm Red Cabbage Slaw

Red cabbage, full of healthy anthocyanins, is a wonderful health food. Brightened with vinegar and lemon juice and sweetened with currants and fennel seed, this warm slaw—*slaw* is the Dutch word for salad—makes a yummy side dish on a dark winter night. Top with toasted walnuts for a little more heft.

SERVES 6

1 small head red cabbage (to yield 3 to 4 cups when shredded)

3 tablespoons olive oil

1 tablespoon fennel seed

½ cup unfiltered apple cider

¼ cup currants or raisins

Juice of ½ lemon

Salt and pepper

Shred cabbage by hand to about ¼-inch thick and 2 inches long.

In a large saucepan, combine about ¼ of the cabbage and the olive oil over medium heat. Keep adding cabbage so that olive oil coats all the pieces.

Cook cabbage, stirring frequently, until it begins to soften, about 10 minutes.

Meanwhile, in a dry, heavy skillet, toast the fennel seeds until just fragrant, about 5 minutes. Set aside.

Add apple cider to the cabbage and heat to simmer. Continue to stir. Add currants. Let cabbage braise until crisp-tender. Add lemon juice. Stir and continue to simmer a few minutes. Season with salt and pepper. Stir in fennel seeds just before serving.

WARM RED CABBAGE SLAW

sugar0607/Fotolia

Preparing food just for youngest grandkids

My sister and I are the youngest of nine grandkids, and my mom's sisters have spoiled us since we were little. My sister loves candied sweet potatoes, so my mom's oldest sister makes them for every holiday dinner. I'm not big on mashed potatoes and gravy, so my mom's baby sister never fails to bring hash brown casserole—just for me. And not to be left out of the spoiling process, my other aunt brings a small dish of creamed peas and a small batch of creamed cabbage for my sister and me. Although we're in our 40s now, we're still the "babies" and are still being spoiled.

And I can't leave my mom out. For Sunday dinners, she makes foods both of us love. Her baked beans are out of this world, and she makes a mean dish of homemade macaroni and cheese.

RaeAnn Lee Roberts
Osage City, Kansas

Baked Okra

We admit that okra can be a challenge to work with, and to consider a comfort food. The problem is usually the slime factor. However, this recipe avoids boiling or braising, which is what renders okra gelatinous. With a crunchy coating and quick baking, the fresh flavor and crisp texture of okra is preserved. Even kids love this dish.

SERVES 8

BAKED OKRA
Brent Hofacker/Fotolia

4 cups sliced okra

1 egg, beaten slightly

1 cup cornmeal

Salt and pepper

Heat oven to 450°F. Cover a baking sheet with aluminum foil; lightly grease the foil. Set aside.

In a medium bowl, mix the okra and egg. Add cornmeal and toss until okra is well coated, adding more cornmeal if necessary. Pour onto the prepared baking sheet. Season with salt and pepper.

Bake for 15 minutes. Remove from oven; turn okra, breaking apart any that may have stuck together. If necessary to prevent sticking, add a small amount of oil and stir. Return to the oven and bake for 15 minutes more, until golden brown.

Scalloped Eggplant

Eggplant is similar to zucchini in that its reputation is bland and watery. As a result, we're always looking for more interesting ways to eat it. This creamy and filling dish fits the bill. This go-to dish will convince you to start growing eggplant in that garden of yours.

SERVES 4

2 cups peeled, cubed eggplant

½ cup coarse bread crumbs, divided

4 tablespoons minced onion

3 ounces grated cheese

1 egg, beaten

½ cup whole milk

2 tablespoons butter

Heat oven to 350°F. Grease a 2-quart casserole dish and set aside.

Cook eggplant in boiling, salted water until tender, about 8 minutes. Drain. Allow to cool slightly.

Pour eggplant into the prepared dish. Sprinkle ¼ cup of the bread crumbs, the onion, and the cheese on top.

In a small bowl, combine the egg and milk; pour over the eggplant mixture. Dot with the butter and sprinkle on the remaining ¼ cup bread crumbs.

Bake for 30 minutes until bubbling and the top is nicely browned.

Stuffed Zucchini

This fun way to eat zucchini deserves a prize. Adding protein and fat via ground meat and cheese turns this garden staple into a delicious vehicle for delivering a healthy dose of folate, potassium, and vitamin A.

SERVES 6

3 medium zucchini, unpeeled

**½ pound ground meat
(beef, turkey, pork, or lamb)**

6 tablespoons cream cheese

1 medium onion, minced

¼ teaspoon salt

¼ teaspoon pepper

½ cup sour cream

Paprika

In a large saucepan, bring water to boiling. Place whole zucchini in boiling water to cover. Do not cover pan. Reduce heat and simmer until nearly tender, 5 to 10 minutes. Cool for 10 minutes.

Meanwhile, brown meat in a skillet. Set aside.

Heat oven to 350°F. Grease a small baking dish and set aside.

Cut each zucchini in half lengthwise; scoop out flesh into a bowl; squeeze out all water from the squash and discard. Mix in cooked meat, cream cheese, onion, salt, and pepper. Spoon filling evenly into shells. Arrange shells in the prepared dish and spoon sour cream evenly over the top of each. Sprinkle each with paprika.

Bake uncovered for 10 minutes. Serve immediately.

STUFFED ZUCCHINI

Karen K. Will

Mashed Rutabagas and Potatoes

Rutabagas are root vegetables often used as to enhance flavor. They have a sweet taste similar to parsnips and turnips and are a traditional ingredient in the New England boiled dinner. This dish is just as flavorful with turnips substituted for the rutabagas.

SERVES 8 TO 10

3 pounds rutabagas, peeled and cut into 2-inch pieces

2 to 2½ pounds russet potatoes, peeled and cut into 2-inch pieces

2 tablespoons butter

⅔ cup milk

¼ teaspoon black pepper

¼ teaspoon nutmeg

Salt

2 teaspoons chopped parsley (optional)

MASHED RUTABAGAS AND POTATOES

anjelagr/Fotolia

In separate saucepans, cook rutabagas and potatoes in salted water. When both are tender, remove from heat and drain. (Rutabagas will take about 30 minutes, and potatoes will take 20 to 25 minutes.)

Mash or purée the rutabagas, then mash the potatoes. Combine the two in a large bowl.

Add butter, milk, pepper, and nutmeg. Beat well. Taste and season with salt. Garnish with chopped parsley.

Taste of new potatoes worth the work

Our family vegetable garden back in southeast Kansas included a potato plot my dad disked with tractor and plow. My brothers and I planted the seed potatoes by hand, and later, once we were old enough, dug them up by hand. I still recall the 7- or 9-potatoes-per-plant results we saw, and I have trouble duplicating that success today. But all of that work was well worth it, the first time my mom had new potatoes on the table: fried chicken, new potatoes and gravy, corn hopefully on the cob, and bread. That was a farmstead staple around late summer and fall, and made all that stooping and then digging well worth it. And today, whether I have a bountiful potato crop or a more meager one, I pull a few new potatoes out early for sides to the season's favorite dishes.

Caleb D. Regan
Lawrence, Kansas

Grandma's Mashed Potatoes

Grandma's secret ingredient in her mashed potatoes was mayonnaise, for a hint of tang—probably because she was fresh out of buttermilk. Use multipurpose Yukon gold, red, white, or russet potatoes for a good mash.

SERVES 6

6 medium potatoes, peeled and cubed

1 tablespoon mayonnaise

½ cup butter

¼ cup whole milk

¼ teaspoon salt

Boil potatoes in a large pot of water until tender. Drain.

Mash and add mayonnaise, butter, milk, and salt. Mix until creamy.

GRANDMA'S MASHED POTATOES

iStockphoto.com/creacart

Can't pick just one

Scalloped potatoes, stuffing, Aunt Mary's hot pickles, Aunt Mary Ethel's corn and oysters, mashed potatoes and gravy—which do I pick? All of them, because I can't choose a favorite side dish.

Holidays were never complete without those hot pickles, homemade from Mary's garden cukes, and we always kept a few back for turkey sandwiches that evening or over the weekend.

I need to find Aunt Mary Ethel's corn and oyster recipe. Now that she is no longer with us, someone needs to bring that delicious dish to the family table.

Jean Teller
Lawrence, Kansas

Horseradish-Garlic Mashed Potatoes

Elevate good mashed potatoes to best-ever mashed potatoes with the additions of garlic and horseradish. Start with a tablespoon or two of horseradish, taste, and add more as you see fit. For a smooth mash, use a food mill or potato ricer; for a chunkier mash, use a manual potato masher.

SERVES 8

3 pounds potatoes (about 8 medium), peeled, cut into 1-inch pieces

4 garlic cloves, peeled, whole

2 teaspoons salt, divided

½ to ¾ cup heavy cream, divided

¼ cup butter, cut into pieces

3 to 4 tablespoons prepared horseradish

¾ teaspoon white pepper

¼ cup chives, snipped, or green onions

In a large saucepan, bring 2 inches of water to boil. Add potatoes, garlic, and ½ teaspoon salt; return to boil. Reduce heat to medium; cover and cook 12 minutes or until potatoes are tender. Drain.

Cook potatoes and garlic over medium-low heat for 1 minute to evaporate excess moisture, stirring occasionally. Remove from heat. Mash potatoes and garlic with electric hand mixer or manual potato masher until smooth.

Add ½ cup cream, butter, horseradish, remaining 1½ teaspoons salt and pepper; stir until blended. Add additional cream, 1 tablespoon at a time, if necessary, for desired consistency. Stir in chives.

HORSERADISH-GARLIC
MASHED POTATOES

iStockphoto.com/Mariha-kitchen

Twice-Baked Potatoes

These are a special treat, and one that kids love. These make a great Meatless Monday dish all on their own, served with a side salad. Mondays suddenly got a whole lot brighter.

SERVES 4 AS MAIN DISH OR 8 AS SIDE DISH

4 medium russet potatoes, washed

1½ pounds cauliflower, washed, green leaves removed

5 tablespoons whole milk, divided

¾ teaspoon salt

¼ teaspoon black pepper

4 ounces sharp cheddar cheese, shredded

Paprika

Heat oven to 350°F. Using a fork, puncture potatoes. Place potatoes directly on oven rack and bake for 40 to 50 minutes, until tender.

Meanwhile, cut cauliflower into 8 pieces and steam until very tender. Transfer cauliflower to the bowl of a food processor or blender. Add 2 tablespoons milk, salt, and pepper. Purée until smooth; mixture will resemble mashed potatoes and make about 1 cup purée. Set aside.

Cut potatoes in half lengthwise. Scoop out the pulp and place in a large mixing bowl, leaving thin shells on the potatoes. Using an electric mixer on the lowest speed, beat potato pulp and remaining 3 tablespoons milk until blended. Add puréed cauliflower mixture and beat until well mixed—do not overbeat. Stir in half of the shredded cheese.

Spoon the mixture evenly into the potato shells. Top with remaining cheese and sprinkle with paprika. Place the potatoes on a baking sheet and bake until cheese melts, about 5 minutes. Serve immediately.

Cheesy New Potatoes with Bacon

The combination of cheese, bacon, and potato is enough to make mouths water. Better yet, this layered casserole calls for no fancy ingredients—just pantry staples—and that means it can be on the table in no time. Drain the potatoes when they are slightly underdone—they'll continue cooking after being taken off the heat as well as in the final bake.

SERVES 6 TO 8

12 medium new potatoes, unpeeled

8 slices bacon, cooked and crumbled

1 cup shredded cheddar cheese

½ cup butter, melted

1 teaspoon salt

¼ teaspoon pepper

Heat oven to 400°F. Grease a 2-quart casserole dish and set aside.

Wash potatoes thoroughly and place in a saucepan. Cover with water and bring to boiling. Reduce heat and cook for 20 minutes, until tender. Drain. Allow potatoes to cool slightly, then cut into ¼-inch-thick slices.

In the prepared dish, layer half of the potatoes, half of the bacon, half of the cheese, ¼ cup butter, ½ teaspoon salt, and ⅛ teaspoon pepper. Repeat layers with remaining ingredients. Bake for 15 minutes, until heated through and lightly browned on top.

Caramel Sweet Potatoes

A holiday gathering—from Thanksgiving through Easter—wouldn't be complete without this classic crowd pleaser. Though technically a vegetable, this dish seems more like dessert to us.

SERVES 8 TO 10

5 medium sweet potatoes

1 teaspoon salt

3 tablespoons all-purpose flour

1 cup packed light brown sugar

2 tablespoons butter

1 cup small marshmallows

½ cup chopped pecans

1 cup half-and-half

Heat oven to 350°F. Grease an 8x11-inch baking dish and set aside.

Wash potatoes thoroughly and place in a saucepan. Cover with water and bring to boiling. Reduce heat and cook for 20 minutes, until tender. Drain. Allow potatoes to cool slightly, then peel and cut crosswise into ½-inch pieces. Arrange potatoes in the prepared dish.

In a small bowl, combine the salt, flour, and brown sugar; sprinkle over the potatoes. Dot with butter and cover with marshmallows and nuts. Pour the half-and-half over all.

Bake for 45 to 50 minutes until bubbling and lightly browned on top.

Baked Stuffed Sweet Potatoes

Loaded with beta carotene, and hence Vitamin A, sweet potatoes are considered a superfood. Adding fat, in the case of butter, only increases our uptake of this important vitamin. Consider the marshmallows optional in this dish—it's just as delicious without them.

SERVES 6 AS A MAIN DISH, 12 AS A SIDE

6 medium sweet potatoes, washed

4 tablespoons butter

1 teaspoon salt

Juice of 1 orange

2 teaspoons lemon juice

½ cup chopped walnuts or pecans

1 cup crushed pineapple

12 large marshmallows, cut into small pieces

Heat oven to 350°F. Using a fork, puncture potatoes. Place potatoes directly on oven rack and bake for 40 to 50 minutes, until tender. Allow to cool for 15 minutes. Increase oven temperature to 375°F.

Slice potatoes lengthwise and scoop out the flesh into a bowl. Mash well and add butter, salt, orange juice, and lemon juice; stir in walnuts and pineapple, mixing thoroughly.

Place sweet potato shells on a baking sheet. Spoon filling evenly into shells and top with marshmallow bits. Bake until marshmallows are melted and lightly browned, 5 to 10 minutes.

Classic Macaroni and Cheese

The cornerstone of comfort food—mac and cheese—satisfies everyone, young and old. This classic calls on mustard, hot pepper sauce, and sharp cheddar to deliver the flavor punch. None of the ingredients overpowers the others, but they all come together in a delightful marriage.

SERVES 4

12 ounces elbow macaroni

3 tablespoons butter

¼ cup diced onion

2 tablespoons flour

2 cups milk

1 teaspoon salt

½ teaspoon pepper

1 to 2 teaspoons hot pepper sauce (such as Tabasco)

1 tablespoon prepared mustard

3 cups shredded sharp cheddar cheese, divided

3 cups coarse bread crumbs

CLASSIC MACARONI AND CHEESE

azurite/Fotolia

Heat oven to 375°F. Butter a 9x9-inch baking dish; set aside.

Cook macaroni according to package instructions or until al dente. Drain, rinse, and set aside.

In a large saucepan, melt butter over medium-high heat. Sauté onion for 2 minutes until soft. Blend in flour, stirring well to incorporate; cook for an additional 2 minutes, stirring constantly. Whisk milk into the butter and flour mixture. Bring to simmer and cook until sauce thickens.

Reduce heat to low; add salt, pepper, hot sauce, and mustard. Stir in 2½ cups cheese. Add cooked macaroni to the cheese sauce and mix well. Pour macaroni mixture into the prepared dish and top with the remaining ½ cup cheese and bread crumbs.

Bake for 25 minutes, until top is golden brown.

Southwestern Mac and Cheese

This flavorful version of macaroni and cheese calls for roasted green chiles, a classic New Mexican ingredient. To roast the chiles, slice them into large strips, removing the seeds and ribs. Place on a baking sheet under the broiler until spottily charred. Transfer the peppers to a bowl and cover with foil for 10 minutes. When cool to the touch, peel the skins off the chiles and slice. Use blue corn tortilla chips for a truly New Mexican dish.

SERVES 6 TO 8

1 pound macaroni, bowtie, or shell noodles

1 teaspoon olive oil

1 clove garlic, pressed

2 tablespoons unsalted butter

1 cup chopped onion

4 tablespoons unbleached flour

2 to 3 large cloves garlic, minced or pressed

4 cups whole milk, divided

1 teaspoon paprika

1 to 1½ teaspoons cumin seed, toasted and ground

Salt and freshly ground black pepper

1 cup grated cheddar cheese, divided

1 cup grated pepper jack cheese, divided

½ cup salsa

½ cup fresh chopped cilantro leaves

4 to 6 large green chiles, roasted, peeled, seeded, and cut into strips

1 cup crushed tortilla chips

Heat oven to 350°F. Butter 2-quart baking dish; set aside.

Cook the pasta al dente. Drain in a colander and toss with olive oil and garlic. Season lightly with salt and freshly ground pepper. Set aside.

In a large sauté pan, melt butter over medium heat. Add onion and cook for 4 to 5 minutes, stirring occasionally. Add flour and stir for about 3 minutes. Add garlic and stir 1 minute more. Add 1 cup milk and stir well to blend. Add remaining milk, whisking to get rid of any lumps. Add paprika, cumin, salt, and pepper.

When sauce is hot, sprinkle in half the cheeses and stir well. When melted, add half the remaining cheeses and stir well. Stir in the salsa and cilantro; remove from heat.

Taste the sauce to see if it needs more salt or pepper, or a little more cumin. Toss the cooked macaroni with the green chiles. Place half the macaroni and chiles in the bottom of the prepared dish; season lightly with salt and pepper. Spread half the sauce over macaroni. Repeat another layer with the remaining macaroni and chiles and sauce; spread the remaining cheese over top. Scatter crushed tortilla chips over top.

Bake for 25 to 30 minutes. Remove from oven and allow the dish to stand for at least 5 minutes before serving.

Mom's Mac and Cheese

We loved Mom's macaroni and cheese—a four-cheese, super rich, extra cheesy version. Elbow macaroni is classic, but Mom always used whatever pasta she had in the pantry—spirals, rigatoni, or bowtie.

SERVES 2 TO 4

MOM'S MAC AND CHEESE
iStockphoto.com/TheCrimsonMonkey

7 ounces elbow macaroni

2 tablespoons butter

2 tablespoons unbleached all-purpose flour

1 teaspoon salt

2 cups milk

1 cup shredded cheddar cheese

1 cup shredded Colby cheese

1 cup shredded Monterey jack cheese

¼ cup Parmesan cheese

2 teaspoons parsley flakes

2 tablespoons bread crumbs

Heat oven to 350°F. Grease a 2-quart casserole dish and set aside.

Cook macaroni according to package directions; drain.

In a large saucepan, melt the butter over medium heat. Stir in the flour and salt; cook for 2 minutes, stirring constantly. Whisk in the milk; cook until thick, about 3 to 5 minutes.

Mix the shredded cheeses together; reserve ¼ cup. Add the cheese to sauce and stir until melted. Stir in the macaroni and parsley. Pour into the prepared dish; top with the reserved cheese and bread crumbs.

Bake for 25 minutes until sauce is bubbling and lightly browned on top. Cool for 5 minutes before serving.

Awesome mac and cheese

I remember coming home from school after walking a million miles uphill in the snow. Nothing warmed me up like the smell of Mom's awesome, amazing macaroni and cheese baking in the oven. No matter how tired from doing an hour of chores in the dark, the savory comfort of that cheesy casserole made it all OK—enough so that I could do it all over again tomorrow.

Hank Will
Scranton, Kansas

Baked Cheese Grits

Plain old grits are comfort food on their own, but add a generous measure of cheese, and this dish is elevated to stick-to-your-ribs status. If your palate leans toward gourmet, top with blue cheese crumbles for a pungent boost of flavor.

SERVES 6

2⅔ cups water

⅔ cup quick-cooking hominy grits

2 tablespoons butter

1½ cups shredded cheddar cheese

2 eggs, beaten

⅛ teaspoon pepper

Heat oven to 350°F. Grease a 2-quart baking dish and set aside.

In a large saucepan, bring water to a full rolling boil; add grits, stir, and return to boiling. Cook, stirring constantly, until very thick, about 6 minutes; remove from heat. Stir in butter, cheese, eggs, and pepper.

Pour into the prepared dish and bake for 40 minutes, until lightly browned.

BAKED CHEESE GRITS

natalikaevsti/Fotolia

Aunt added love to her cooking

One of my fondest memories growing up was spending the week at my aunt's house. She had a huge farm, and there were so many fun things to do and explore. I, being a tomboy, preferred spending my time outdoors and helping with farm chores, but I also helped my aunt in the kitchen. She was an amazing cook, and I loved wearing one of her homemade aprons. You couldn't help but feel the warmth and love she put into her fried chicken, her homemade pies, and her famous cinnamon rolls.

Ilene Reid
Burlingame, Kansas

Mother-in-Law Dressing

Lightly seasoned with sage, this is a wonderfully versatile side dish to accompany any meat.

SERVES 6 TO 8

MOTHER-IN-LAW DRESSING

Brent Hofacker/Fotolia

4 cups dry bread crumbs

½ teaspoon salt

2 teaspoons baking powder

1 teaspoon dried sage

½ teaspoon black pepper

2 cups milk, scalded

4 tablespoons butter

1 cup chopped celery

1 cup chopped onion

1 egg, beaten

½ cup chicken broth

Heat oven to 350°F. Grease a 2-quart casserole dish and set aside.

In a large bowl, combine bread crumbs, salt, baking powder, sage, and pepper. Pour milk over mixture; stir to moisten. Let stand for 20 minutes.

In a large skillet, melt butter over medium-high heat. Add celery and onions and sauté until onions are tender.

Add sautéed vegetables and egg to the bread crumb mixture and mix well. Pour into the prepared dish. Pour the broth evenly over the casserole. Cover and bake for 1 hour until hot.

Wild Mushroom Dressing

Resplendent with myriad vegetables, herbs, and pork, this dressing makes a fine main dish on its own.

SERVES 10-12

¼ cup butter

8 ounces shiitake mushrooms, cleaned and sliced

1 cup chopped onion

¾ cup chopped green bell pepper

¾ cup chopped yellow bell pepper

½ cup chopped celery

1 tablespoon chicken-flavored instant bouillon

8 cups dry light rye bread cubes (about 16 slices)

¼ pound prosciutto or ham, chopped

½ cup water

½ teaspoon dried tarragon leaves

⅛ teaspoon black pepper

Heat oven to 350°F. Grease a 4-quart casserole dish and set aside.

In a large skillet, melt the butter over medium-high heat. Add the mushrooms, onion, peppers, celery, and bouillon, and cook until vegetables are tender.

In a large bowl, combine the bread cubes, ham, water, tarragon, and pepper. Stir in the sautéed vegetables and mix well.

Spoon the stuffing into the prepared dish. Cover and bake for 30 minutes, until hot. Refrigerate leftovers.

Waldorf Stuffing

Experts say to safely roast a stuffed turkey, keep the bird to 15 pounds or smaller, and microwave the stuffing on high for 6 to 8 minutes before stuffing the turkey. To prepare this dish as a casserole, add 2 teaspoons chicken broth or water for each cup of stuffing and bake at 325°F for 25 to 30 minutes.

MAKES 12 CUPS (STUFFING FOR A 12- TO 14-POUND TURKEY)

¾ cup (1½ sticks) butter

1½ cups chopped celery

1½ cups chopped unpeeled red cooking apples (about 2 large)

¾ cup coarsely chopped walnuts

1 teaspoon salt

¼ teaspoon black pepper

6 cups toasted whole wheat bread cubes

6 cups toasted white bread cubes

2 cups chicken or turkey broth

2 eggs, beaten

WALDORF STUFFING

iStockphoto.com/Nicole Branan

In a 4-quart Dutch oven, melt the butter over medium-high heat. Add the celery and sauté until tender, about 5 minutes.

Stir in the apples, nuts, salt, and pepper. Add the bread cubes and mix well.

In a bowl, combine the broth and eggs. Pour over the bread mixture and toss to coat.

Spoon the stuffing into the turkey and roast accordingly.

Hamburger Gravy

This gravy is a dish all in itself. Cook the meat and onions, then make the gravy in the same pan, and serve the meaty gravy over biscuits, potatoes, or rice for an easy, hearty supper. For a beefy mushroom gravy, add 1 teaspoon Worcestershire sauce and some fresh mushrooms.

SERVES 4

1 pound ground beef

½ cup chopped onion

3 tablespoons unbleached all-purpose flour

1 tablespoon beef-flavored instant bouillon

2 tablespoons steak sauce

2 cups milk

In a large skillet over medium-high heat, cook ground beef and onion, breaking meat into crumbles, until beef is cooked through.

Stir in the flour, bouillon, and steak sauce; cook for 3 minutes, stirring constantly. Gradually stir in the milk, whisking to break up any clumps. Cook, stirring frequently, for 4 to 6 minutes, until mixture boils and thickens.

This is gravy?

When I first married in 1972, I wasn't a very good cook. One evening for supper I made gravy and something. We were eating, and someone knocked at the front door, which wasn't used by family or friends. It was an insurance salesman. My hubby and I sat on the couch facing the kitchen table. My sister came in the back door right into the kitchen. It seemed a lifetime dragged by as the salesman talked when I happened to look up and see my sister holding the gravy bowl upsidedown and the spoon didn't fall out. It was captured by the hardened gravy.

Janice Keener
Linden, Texas

Chicken Gravy

Thick, milky white gravy served over chicken or turkey just feels right in your mouth. Use the chicken drippings from a roasted chicken or turkey to start this gravy. Whisk, whisk, whisk to remove all the lumps. Experiment with Wondra, an instant flour that is low in protein and finely ground and doesn't require the same long cooking process as ordinary flour to dissolve in a liquid and thicken it. Our grandmothers often used this to produce smooth, lump-free gravy.

MAKES 1 CUP

3 tablespoons fat from frying pan or baking dish

2 tablespoons unbleached all-purpose flour

1 cup milk

Salt and pepper

After pan-frying your chicken, pour off the fat from skillet into a measuring cup, leaving the brown bits in the pan. Return 3 tablespoons of fat to the pan.

Whisk in the flour and cook over medium heat, stirring and scraping brown bits from the bottom of the pan, until the flour is lightly browned. Remove from heat. Gradually whisk in the milk.

Return the skillet to heat, and cook, stirring constantly, until thickened. If the gravy is too thick, add a little additional milk. Season with salt and pepper. Serve immediately.

CHICKEN GRAVY

msheldrake/Fotolia

Chapter 8
Cookies, Bars, and Candies

THE PRIDE OF ANY country cook is the ability to wow and delight eaters with superb baked goods: cookies, brownies, and bars. All the little tips that turn ordinary cookies and brownies into real stunners are what makes the difference. From properly creaming your sugar and fat (don't be stingy—beat for at least 3 minutes) to flattening your cookie balls with the bottom of a drinking glass, all the tricks of the trade can be practiced here.

Homemade candies are the hallmark of an old-fashioned holiday. Forget the store-bought candies perfectly turned out in a factory somewhere. Rekindle the time-honored traditions of candy making by hosting a day of it; invite your best friend, sister, or children, and create your own tradition by turning out your favorite delicacies. Package your treats in antique tins, baking vessels, or blue Ball jars for a thoughtful gift.

Sweet treats beg for your own creative touch. Use these recipes as a launching pad and experiment with different chocolates, chips, extracts, nuts, and other additions to come up with your own specialties; just keep proportions the same, and it's hard to go wrong.

Soft Sugar Cookies

The perfect combination of chewy and crunchy, these sugar cookies are classic and make a thoughtful gift for every occasion, from birthdays to holidays. These cookies are fun to make, so enlist the kids to help.

MAKES 3 DOZEN

SOFT SUGAR COOKIES
istockphotos.com/adlifemarketing

2½ cups granulated sugar, divided

1 cup lard or butter (or a combination), softened

2 eggs, beaten

1½ teaspoons baking soda

2 teaspoons baking powder

2 teaspoons cream of tartar

1 scant teaspoon salt

5 cups unbleached, all-purpose flour

1 cup milk

2 teaspoons vanilla

Heat oven to 350°F. Line two baking sheets with parchment paper and set aside.

In a large bowl, cream 2 cups of the sugar with the lard or butter. Beat in the eggs.

In a separate bowl, sift the baking soda, baking powder, cream of tartar, salt, and flour together. Add half of the dry ingredients to the creamed mixture. Blend in the milk, vanilla, and remaining dry ingredients.

Place the remaining ½ cup sugar in a wide bowl or pan.

Roll the dough into 1½-inch balls with slightly wet hands, then roll in the sugar and place on the prepared baking sheets. Using the bottom of a drinking glass, flatten each ball.

Bake for 10 to 12 minutes, until lightly golden.

Sugar cookie memories

When I was a little girl, every year all of the family would gather at our Aunt Brenda's on Christmas Eve. At the time, my little sister and I were the youngest girls. We couldn't wait to get to Aunt Brenda's. She would have tons of sugar cookie dough waiting for us, and my little sister, Aunt Brenda, and I would get out all the Christmas cookie cutters. For what seemed like hours (and probably was), we would cut out and bake and decorate sugar cookies.

The patience Aunt Brenda had with us was amazing; she is like a grandmother to me and very dear to my heart. Now that we are grown and have moved away with families of our own, we don't always make it to Aunt Brenda's on Christmas Eve, but I always remember those times as I watch my own children cut out and decorate sugar cookies. I hope that she knows just what a wonderful influence she is and how much I treasure those memories.

Angela Jones
via Facebook

Giant Chocolate Peanut Butter Cookies

These café-style, oversize cookies are delightful. To achieve the craggy top, you'll need to master the technique of pulling apart a dough ball and mashing it back together just so. After a few turns, you'll get the hang of it. For variation, make double-chocolate-chip cookies by substituting ⅓ cup cocoa powder for an equal part of flour, and substitute ½ cup semisweet chocolate chips for the peanut butter chips.

MAKES 18 COOKIES

2 cups unbleached all-purpose flour

½ teaspoon baking soda

½ teaspoon salt

1½ sticks unsalted butter, melted and cooled

1 cup packed dark brown sugar

½ cup granulated sugar

1 large egg plus 1 egg yolk

2 teaspoons vanilla extract

1 cup semisweet chocolate chips

½ cup peanut butter chips

Adjust two oven racks to upper-middle and lower-middle positions. Heat oven to 325°F. Line two baking sheets with parchment paper and set aside.

In a small bowl, stir together flour, baking soda, and salt; set aside.

In a large bowl, combine butter and sugars using an electric mixer on medium speed, beating for at least 3 minutes, or until sugar is no longer grainy. Beat in the egg, egg yolk, and vanilla until thoroughly combined, about 1 minute.

Add the dry ingredients all at once and beat on low speed until just combined. Stir in the chocolate and peanut butter chips. Refrigerate the dough in the bowl for 15 to 20 minutes, until well chilled.

Using a ¼-cup measuring cup, scoop out dough to a scant ¼ cup. Tap out dough into your hand and tear it in half. Press two flat sides together, with torn edges facing up. Make sure the cookie halves are stuck together, but don't smooth them. Place 6 cookies, evenly spaced, on prepared baking

GIANT CHOCOLATE
PEANUT BUTTER COOKIES

Karen K. Will

sheets. Return unused dough to refrigerator between batches.

Bake for 17 minutes, rotating sheets upper to lower, front to back, halfway through baking time. Cool for 20 minutes on baking sheets before removing to wire racks to cool completely.

Frosted Rhubarb Cookies

When we think of rhubarb dishes, gooey pies, cobblers, and crisps come to mind. But these cookies are a refreshing take on this culinary wild child. The delicious cream-cheese frosting turns these cookies into miniature cakes. For a lower-sugar, lower-calorie treat, omit the frosting—the cookies are just as tasty without it.

MAKES 4 DOZEN

FROSTED RHUBARB COOKIES

Lori Dunn

Cookies:

1 cup lard or butter, softened

1½ cups packed brown sugar

2 eggs

3 cups unbleached all-purpose flour

1 teaspoon baking soda

½ teaspoon salt

1½ cups diced fresh or frozen rhubarb (see note)

¾ cup flaked coconut

Frosting:

1 small package (3 ounces) cream cheese, softened

1 tablespoon butter, softened

1½ cups confectioner's sugar

3 teaspoons vanilla extract

For cookies: Heat oven to 350°F. Grease baking sheets or line with parchment paper; set aside.

In a large bowl, cream the lard or butter and brown sugar. Beat in the eggs.

In a separate bowl, combine the flour, baking soda, and salt; gradually add to the creamed mixture and beat until well combined. Fold in the rhubarb and coconut.

Drop by rounded tablespoonfuls, 1 inch apart, onto the prepared baking sheets. Bake for 10 to 14 minutes, until golden brown. Cool for 1 minute before removing to wire racks to cool completely.

For frosting: In a small mixing bowl, beat cream cheese and butter until fluffy. Beat in the confectioner's sugar and vanilla. Spread over the cooled cookies.

Note: If using frozen rhubarb, measure rhubarb while still frozen. Then thaw completely and drain in a colander, but do not press out the liquid.

Snickerdoodles

These cookies are an old standby comfort food, a staple of Christmases past. Snickerdoodles are simply sugar cookies rolled in cinnamon sugar, but where does the odd name come from? Some sources claim the name is of German origin, a corruption of the word *Schneckennudeln*, a kind of pastry whose name translates to "snail noodles." Others attribute the name to nonsense, with no particular meaning, originating from a New England tradition of whimsical cookie names.

MAKES 3 DOZEN

1 cup butter or lard, or combination

1½ cups plus 2 tablespoons granulated sugar, divided

2 eggs

2¾ cups sifted unbleached, all-purpose flour

2 teaspoons cream of tartar

1 teaspoon baking soda

½ teaspoon salt

2 teaspoons cinnamon

Heat oven to 400°F.

In a large bowl, cream the butter or lard with 1½ cups sugar. Beat in the eggs.

In a separate bowl, sift the flour, cream of tartar, soda, and salt together; add to the creamed mixture and beat until well combined. Roll dough into walnut-size balls.

Combine remaining 2 tablespoons sugar and cinnamon; roll the balls in the mixture and place them about 2 inches apart on ungreased baking sheets.

Bake for 8 to 10 minutes, until light brown but still soft. Cookies will puff up in the oven but then flatten out and have crinkled tops.

SNICKERDOODLES

istockphotos.com/1MoreCreative

Peanut Butter Cookies

Chewy, nutty, and emblazoned with that familiar crisscross pattern, these peanut butter cookies are a protein-packed treat. Use creamy or crunchy peanut butter for variation; for chewier cookies, bake at 300°F for 15 minutes. Serve with a tall glass of milk, of course.

MAKES 4 DOZEN

PEANUT BUTTER COOKIES
istockphotos.com/jrennison

1 cup butter, softened

1 cup granulated sugar

1 cup packed brown sugar

1 cup creamy peanut butter

2 eggs

2½ cups unbleached, all-purpose flour

1½ teaspoons baking soda

1 teaspoon baking powder

½ teaspoon salt

In a large bowl, cream the butter for 2 minutes. Add the sugars and beat for 2 more minutes. Mix in the peanut butter and eggs.

In a separate bowl, combine the flour, baking soda, baking powder, and salt. Stir the dry ingredients into the creamed mixture.

Wrap dough in plastic wrap and refrigerate for at least 3 hours.

Heat oven to 375°F.

Shape the dough into 1¼-inch balls. Place about 3 inches apart on ungreased baking sheets. Flatten with a fork, making a crisscross pattern.

Bake for 9 to 10 minutes, until light brown. Cool on baking sheets for a minute, then transfer to a wire rack to cool completely.

What is mincemeat?

Among the holiday treats from my childhood were cookies shaped in half moons, the sweet dough pressed around a dollop of mincemeat and puffed to a golden brown.

The cookies were favorites in our household; although for me, the appeal was probably more the pie crust dough than the sweet mincemeat inside. Mom used jarred mincemeat from the grocery store, and I don't think I realized real mincemeat actually contained meat until I was grown and away from home. I have a feeling that had Mom used real mincemeat, those cookies would not hold such a place of fondness in my memory.

Jean Teller
Lawrence, Kansas

Cream Cheese Chocolate Chip Cookies

Cream cheese in cookie batter? You won't know until you try it, but the cream cheese makes these cookies creamy and dense—more substantial than an ordinary cookie. Add pecans and lemon extract, and you end up with a surprisingly delicious morsel.

MAKES 4 DOZEN

CREAM CHEESE CHOCOLATE CHIP COOKIES

istockphotos.com/ejwhite

1 cup butter, softened

1 cup granulated sugar

1 package (3 ounces) cream cheese, at room temperature

2 eggs

1 teaspoon vanilla

½ teaspoon lemon extract

2½ cups unbleached, all-purpose flour, spooned into cup

1 teaspoon baking powder

½ teaspoon baking soda

1 cup coarsely chopped pecans or walnuts

1 cup semisweet chocolate chips

Heat oven to 350°F. Lightly grease two baking sheets or line with parchment paper; set aside.

In a large bowl, cream butter well; add sugar, beating until smooth and fluffy. Blend in cream cheese, eggs, vanilla, and lemon extract.

In a separate bowl, mix together the flour, baking powder, and baking soda. Add to the creamed mixture and mix well. Fold in pecans and chocolate chips.

Drop dough by teaspoonfuls onto prepared baking sheets. Bake for 12 to 15 minutes, until golden brown. Cool on wire racks.

Thin chocolate chip cookies hit the spot

Chocolate chip cookies, along with homemade chili, are the two dishes that most make me recall my Grandma Mary's kitchen. She loved to prepare them for her grandsons, and being a Depression-era single mother of three kids, she sure made those two foods stretch. Despite being slightly watered-down, I'll never forget how tasty those thin cookies were.

Caleb D. Regan
Lawrence, Kansas

Peanut Butter Butterscotch Chip Cookies

Peanut butter and butterscotch—who doesn't love these flavors? These crunchy, caramely cookies are perfect for a tailgate party on a cool autumn day. Everyone will be reaching for seconds and asking for the recipe.

MAKES 3 DOZEN

1 cup lard or butter, softened

1 cup creamy peanut butter

1 cup granulated sugar

1 cup packed brown sugar

1 egg

2 cups unbleached, all-purpose flour, sifted

¾ teaspoon salt

¾ teaspoon baking soda

1½ tablespoons milk

1 package (10 ounces) butterscotch chips

PEANUT BUTTER
BUTTERSCOTCH COOKIES

kmjohnson/Fotolia

Heat oven to 350°F.

In a large bowl, cream together the lard or butter, peanut butter, and sugars. Add the egg, flour, and salt, mixing well. Dissolve the baking soda in the milk; add to the creamed mixture and mix until well combined. Stir in the butterscotch chips.

Roll dough into 1-inch balls and place on an ungreased baking sheet. Flatten the balls with your hand and bake for about 10 minutes, until golden brown.

Rich and Chewy Chocolate Brownies

These brownies are reminiscent of restaurant desserts that come dolloped with fudge sauce, ice cream, and whipped cream. A really decadent chocolate treat, serve these for a special birthday at home. The guest of honor will be delighted.

MAKES 2 DOZEN BROWNIES

RICH AND CHEWY
CHOCOLATE BROWNIES
istockphotos.com/Nathan_David_Hall

¾ cup granulated sugar

½ cup (1 stick) butter

2 tablespoons water

2 bars (8 ounces each) dark chocolate baking bar, chopped

2 large eggs

2 teaspoons vanilla extract

1 cup unbleached all-purpose flour

¼ teaspoon baking soda

¼ teaspoon salt

½ cup chopped nuts, optional

Heat oven to 350°F. Grease a 9x13-inch baking pan; set aside.

In a large saucepan, heat the sugar, butter, and water over medium-high heat until the mixture boils, stirring once. Remove from heat.

Add the chocolate and stir until melted. Stir in the eggs, one at a time, until incorporated. Stir in the vanilla extract. Add the flour, baking soda, and salt; stir well. Stir in the nuts.

Pour batter into the prepared baking pan. Bake for 16 to 20 minutes, until a wooden toothpick inserted in the center comes out still slightly sticky. Cool in pan on a wire rack. Cut into 24 squares.

Peanut Butter Brownies

We love peanut butter not only for its nutty flavor, but for the protein it adds to dishes like these.

MAKES 80

6 eggs

3 cups granulated sugar

1½ cups brown sugar, firmly packed

1 cup creamy or crunchy peanut butter

½ cup lard or butter, softened

1 tablespoon vanilla

4 cups flour

1½ tablespoons baking powder

1½ teaspoons salt

½ cup chopped peanuts

Heat oven to 350°F. Lightly grease two 15½x10½x1-inch baking sheets, or three 13x9x2-inch pans, and set aside.

In a large bowl, combine the eggs, sugars, peanut butter, lard or butter, and vanilla; blend thoroughly using an electric mixer. Gradually add flour, baking powder, and salt; mix until smooth.

Spread the dough into the prepared pans. Sprinkle nuts over the top and bake for 20 minutes, until a toothpick inserted near the center comes out clean.

Cool in the pans. Cut into 80 bars.

Chocolate Chip Blondies

The brown sugar caramelizes for a butterscotch flavor in these blond brownies, and the chips on top add just the right touch of chocolate. For a slightly more sophisticated flavor, try using bittersweet chocolate chips in place of semisweet. For variation, substitute vanilla chips for the chocolate and add nuts to the topping.

MAKES 24

CHOCOLATE CHIP BLONDIES
istockphotos.com/boblin

⅔ cup butter, softened

2 cups packed brown sugar

2 tablespoons hot water

2 eggs

2 teaspoons vanilla

2 cups unbleached, all-purpose flour

1 teaspoon baking powder

¼ teaspoon baking soda

1 teaspoon salt

½ cup semisweet chocolate chips

Heat oven to 350°F.

In a large bowl, cream the butter and sugar. Add the hot water, eggs, and vanilla, beating well. Add the flour, baking powder, baking soda, and salt, beating until well combined.

Spread the batter into a greased 9x13-inch pan. Sprinkle the chocolate chips on top.

Bake for 25 to 30 minutes. Cool slightly and cut into 24 squares.

London Bars

A home cook from across the pond sent us this recipe.

MAKES 24

½ cup butter, softened

1½ cups packed brown sugar, divided

1 cup plus 3 tablespoons unbleached, all-purpose flour, divided

2 eggs

½ teaspoon salt

1 cup chopped nuts

1½ cups unsweetened shredded coconut

1 teaspoon vanilla

Heat the oven to 375°F.

In a large bowl, cream the butter; add ½ cup of the brown sugar and 1 cup of the flour; mix thoroughly. Spread in a 9x9x2-inch baking dish. Bake for 10 minutes.

Meanwhile, beat eggs until light. Add the remaining 1 cup of brown sugar, the remaining 3 tablespoons flour, and salt; mix well. Stir in the nuts, coconut, and vanilla, mixing well.

Once the baked layer has cooled slightly, spread the egg mixture over it. Bake for 20 to 30 minutes longer, until a toothpick inserted near the center comes out clean. Cool completely before cutting into bars.

Nut Brittle Cookie Bars

A cross between a bar cookie and a peanut brittle, these treats truly satisfy the nonchocolate lovers. As a healthy alternative, substitute agave nectar or honey for the corn syrup.

MAKES 2 DOZEN

1⅔ cups unbleached, all-purpose flour

1½ cups plus 2 tablespoons granulated sugar, divided

¾ teaspoon baking powder

1 cup (2 sticks) butter, divided

1 egg, slightly beaten

½ cup plus 2 tablespoons evaporated milk, divided

1⅔ cups (10-ounce package) peanut butter chips, divided

½ cup light corn syrup

1½ cups dry roasted, unsalted peanuts

NUT BRITTLE COOKIE BARS

Chas53/Fotolia

Heat oven to 375°F.

In a large bowl, stir together the flour, 2 tablespoons of the sugar, and the baking powder. Using a pastry blender, cut in ½ cup (1 stick) butter until the mixture forms coarse crumbs. Stir in the egg and 2 tablespoons evaporated milk; mix until mixture holds together. Press dough evenly into the bottom and up the sides of a 15½x10½x1-inch jellyroll pan.

Bake for 8 to 10 minutes, until golden; cool in the pan on a wire rack. Sprinkle 1 cup of chips over crust.

In a large saucepan, combine remaining 1½ cups sugar, remaining 1 stick of butter, remaining ½ cup evaporated milk, and corn syrup. Cook over medium heat, stirring constantly, until mixture boils; stir in the peanuts. Continue cooking and stirring until mixture reaches 240°F on a candy thermometer, or soft ball stage.

Remove pan from heat and immediately spoon over the baked layer. Do not spread—it will spread during baking. Bake for 12 to 15 minutes, until filling is caramel colored. Remove from the oven and immediately sprinkle the remaining ⅔ cup chips over the top. Cool completely in the pan on a wire rack. Cut into bars.

Frosted Peanut Butter Bars

These creamy, nutty bars are extra special with the frosting on top. Use pure lard for superior mouth feel or butter for a rich taste.

MAKES 16

Bars:

½ **cup lard or butter, softened**

½ **cup granulated sugar**

½ **cup packed brown sugar**

⅓ **cup creamy peanut butter**

½ **teaspoon vanilla extract**

1 **egg**

¼ **cup milk**

1 **cup unbleached all-purpose flour**

½ **teaspoon baking soda**

½ **teaspoon salt**

1 **cup oatmeal**

Frosting:

½ **cup butter, softened**

1 **cup creamy peanut butter**

4 **cups confectioner's sugar**

¼ **cup cream**

Heat oven to 350°F.

To make bars: in a large bowl, cream the shortening with the sugars. Add the peanut butter, vanilla, egg, and milk. Sift in the flour, baking soda, and salt. Add the oatmeal and mix well.

Spread the mixture into a 13x9x2-inch baking pan. Bake for 20 to 25 minutes, until golden brown. Cool thoroughly.

To make frosting: in a large bowl, beat the butter and peanut butter until light and fluffy. Slowly beat in 2 cups confectioner's sugar. Mix in the cream. Beat in remaining powdered sugar. If necessary, add a little more cream until frosting reaches a good spreading consistency. Spread over the cooled bars and cut into squares.

Lemon Cookie Bars

Lemon bars make us think of our grandmothers. Tart and sweet, gooey lemon bars sprinkled with confectioner's sugar are a standby dessert and always a crowd pleaser—among old and young alike.

MAKES 24

½ cup butter, softened

Pinch of salt

¼ cup confectioners' sugar

1 cup plus 2 tablespoons unbleached all-purpose flour, divided

2 eggs

1 cup granulated sugar

3 tablespoons lemon juice

Zest from 1 lemon

Heat oven to 350°F.

In a large bowl, mix the butter, salt, confectioner's sugar, and 1 cup of the flour together; press into a 9x13-inch pan. Bake for 15 minutes, until crust is lightly browned. Cool.

In a separate bowl, beat the eggs, granulated sugar, remaining 2 tablespoons of flour, and the lemon juice and zest together; pour into the cooled crust.

Bake for another 25 minutes, until set. Once cool, dust with additional confectioner's sugar. Cut into bite-size squares.

LEMON COOKIE BARS

istockphotos.com/rjgrant

Frosted Coffee Bars

Coffee as an ingredient in baked goods serves to elevate the taste just so and give a slightly sophisticated edge to the dish. The double hit—both in the batter and the frosting—really delivers the goods for coffee lovers. Make these for your next book club meeting.

MAKES 2 DOZEN

Bars:

1 cup packed brown sugar

1 cup granulated sugar

1 cup lard or butter, softened

3 eggs

3 cups sifted unbleached all-purpose flour

1 teaspoon cinnamon

½ teaspoon ginger

½ teaspoon nutmeg

1 teaspoon baking powder

1 teaspoon baking soda

½ teaspoon salt

1 cup strong coffee, cold

1 teaspoon vanilla, divided

½ cup nuts (optional)

Frosting:

4 tablespoons butter

¼ cup hot coffee

2 cups confectioner's sugar

Pinch of salt

½ teaspoon vanilla

Heat oven to 325°F.

To make bars: in a large bowl, cream together the sugars and lard or butter; add eggs and beat until fluffy.

Sift together the flour, cinnamon, ginger, nutmeg, baking powder, baking soda, and salt. Starting with the flour mixture, add alternately with the cold coffee to creamed mixture, mixing well after each addition, and ending with the flour mixture. Fold in vanilla and nuts.

Pour into two 9x13-inch baking pans and bake for 25 to 30 minutes.

To make frosting: melt the butter in a saucepan. Add the hot coffee and stir. Whisk in the confectioner's sugar, salt, and vanilla; whisk until smooth. Cool slightly and spread over the baked bars. Cut into 24 squares.

Frosted Pumpkin Bars

At *Grit*, we believe in (and love) endless variations on a theme. Whether that's bar cookies or raising chickens, we can never get enough. The addition of pumpkin to this recipe delivers a healthy dose of beta carotene—an added bonus.

MAKES 36

Bars:

4 eggs

½ cup butter, melted

½ cup sour cream

2 cups granulated sugar

2 teaspoons cinnamon

1 cup pumpkin purée

½ teaspoon salt

2 cups unbleached, all-purpose flour

1 teaspoon baking powder

1 teaspoon baking soda

Frosting:

3 ounces cream cheese, softened

6 tablespoons butter, softened

3 cups confectioner's sugar

1 teaspoon vanilla

1 teaspoon milk

To make bars: Heat oven to 350°F. Grease an 11x15x1-inch sheet pan and set aside.

In a large bowl, beat the eggs; add the melted butter and sour cream, sugar, cinnamon, and pumpkin.

In a separate small bowl, combine the salt, flour, baking powder, and baking soda; add to pumpkin mixture, mixing well. Pour into the prepared pan.

Bake for 25 minutes, until a toothpick inserted near the center comes out clean.

Frosting: In a large bowl, cream together the cream cheese and butter. Gradually add the confectioner's sugar, vanilla, and milk; beating well. Spread frosting over the baked mixture while still warm. Allow to cool before cutting into bars.

Peanut Butter Bars

These bars are similar to the good old peanut butter cup candy sold in markets all over the world. But, these are better because they're homemade with simple ingredients. Knock 'em out with this favorite, time-tested combination.

MAKES 12

5.5 ounces graham cracker crumbs

1 cup butter (2 sticks), softened

1 cup creamy peanut butter

1 pound confectioner's sugar

2 cups semisweet chocolate chips, melted

Butter a 9-inch-square pan and set aside.

In a large bowl, beat together the butter and peanut butter. Add the confectioner's sugar and graham cracker crumbs, beating until smooth.

Press mixture into the prepared pan. Spread melted chocolate over the top. Cover and chill in the refrigerator until firm. Cut into 12 squares.

Chocolate Peanut Butter Truffles with Sea Salt

Chocolate truffles are a treat, usually reserved for birthdays or other gift-giving occasions. Making them yourself is remarkably easy, and when you put a little care into the process, they will look and taste every bit as good as the chocolatier version. These truffles qualify as dangerous, so be careful when sampling. The pinch of sea salt pushes the taste over the top.

MAKES 3 DOZEN

12 ounces crunchy peanut butter

2 sticks butter, softened

1 pound confectioners' sugar

1 teaspoon vanilla

12 ounces bittersweet chocolate chips

Flaked sea salt

In a large bowl, mix together the peanut butter, butter, confectioner's sugar, and vanilla, using your hands or a large rubber spatula. Roll into 1-ounce balls (use a kitchen scale to approximate the size) and place on baking sheets lined with wax paper. Place sheets in the freezer for 1 hour.

Melt the chocolate in double boiler or microwave. Using a spoon, dunk truffle into chocolate and roll around to coat all sides. Using the same spoon, lift it from the chocolate and allow the excess to drip off. Roll it onto a clean spoon and then onto a baking sheet lined with wax paper. Have a helper immediately sprinkle a pinch of sea salt on top. Work quickly and carefully for the best results.

Cool truffles for several hours before disturbing.

CHOCOLATE PEANUT BUTTER TRUFFLES WITH SEA SALT

Karen K. Will

Pecan Pralines

Pralines are a specialty of New Orleans and the South. They originated with French settlers in Louisiana, who found abundant sugar cane and pecan trees. Countless praline recipes, formulations, and textures exist, but they're all basically the melding of burnt sugar and crunchy nuts.

MAKES 3 DOZEN

PECAN PRALINES
istockphotos.com/Warren_Price

3 cups granulated sugar, divided

¾ cup milk

2 tablespoons butter

1 cup chopped pecans

1 teaspoon vanilla extract

Butter two baking sheets and set aside.

In a large saucepan, combine 2 cups of sugar with the milk; bring to a boil and let it boil gently.

Meanwhile, place the remaining 1 cup of sugar in a heavy pan. Cook over medium heat, stirring constantly, until caramelized and smooth. Stir the caramelized sugar slowly into the first mixture, stirring constantly. Cook until it forms a soft ball (235°F) when dropped into cold water. Remove from heat. Stir in butter and cool until lukewarm.

Add pecans and vanilla; beat until creamy. Drop carefully by spoonfuls onto prepared baking sheets. Cool thoroughly before transferring to an airtight container.

Milk Chocolate Almond Clusters

This has got to be one of the easiest recipes for candy, but nonetheless tasty and satisfying. Substitute different chips—bittersweet, semisweet, butterscotch—and different nuts for endless variations. These clusters are a great addition to your holiday cookie tins.

2 cups (1 12-ounce package) milk chocolate chips

¼ cup (½ stick) butter, cut into pieces

1½ cups slivered almonds

¼ cup vanilla baking chips, melted (optional)

Line two baking sheets with waxed paper and set aside.

Combine chocolate chips and butter in a microwave-safe bowl; microwave on medium power for 2 minutes, then stir. Microwave for 30 to 60 seconds longer, stirring every 30 seconds, until melted and smooth. Quickly stir in almonds.

Using 2 spoons, drop mixture into 36 mounds on prepared baking sheets. Drizzle with melted vanilla chips, if desired. Refrigerate, uncovered, until firm, about 40 minutes. Transfer to a container with a tight-fitting lid. Store in the refrigerator.

Buttery Brittle

Salty nuts encased in caramelized sugar—we're not sure if it gets much better than that. Though this recipe gives microwave instructions, it can easily be made the old-fashioned way—on the stovetop, using a candy thermometer.

MAKES 2 POUNDS

2 cups granulated sugar

1 cup light corn syrup

⅓ cup water

2½ cups coarsely chopped salted peanuts or cashews

½ cup (1 stick) butter

2 teaspoons baking soda

Grease two baking sheets and set aside.

In a large microwave-safe bowl, combine the sugar, syrup, and water; microwave on high for 8 to 10 minutes, stirring twice, until soft ball stage (235°F) is reached. Stir in the nuts.

Microwave on high for 10 to 12 minutes, until hard crack stage (300° to 310°F) is reached. Stir in the butter and baking soda.

Pour half of the mixture on each baking sheet, spreading to ¼-inch thickness. Cool completely at room temperature. Break into pieces.

Store between sheets of waxed paper in an airtight container in the refrigerator for up to 1 month.

BUTTERY BRITTLE

Michael Ballard/Fotolia

Smoky Almond Chocolate Bark

Talk about easy—simply heat the chocolate in the microwave or atop a double boiler, stir in the nuts, and you're done. Makes a great addition to your fall tailgating spread.

MAKES ½ POUND

SMOKY ALMOND CHOCOLATE BARK

Nestle

8 ounces dark chocolate baking bar, broken into small pieces

½ cup coarsely chopped smoke-flavored almonds, divided

⅛ teaspoon coarse sea salt

Line an 8-inch square baking pan with wax paper.

In a microwave-safe bowl, microwave chocolate, uncovered, on high power for 45 seconds; stir. If needed, microwave an additional 10 to 15 seconds, in intervals, stirring just until melted. Stir in ¼ cup of the almonds.

Pour into the prepared baking pan and sprinkle with remaining almonds. Tap pan to spread the chocolate and settle nuts. Sprinkle with sea salt.

Refrigerate for 1 hour, until firm. Remove from the pan and break into pieces. Store in an airtight container at room temperature.

Never-Fail Divinity

Divinity is a divine, old-time favorite, yet it isn't the easiest thing to make. Our advice? Become the eager student of an elderly person well versed in candy making. You'll both come away with more than a box of sweet treats. To give as a gift, wrap individual candies in cut-up sheets of wax paper.

MAKES 2 POUNDS

2 cups granulated sugar

½ cup light corn syrup

½ cup hot water

¼ teaspoon salt

2 large egg whites

1 teaspoon vanilla extract

½ cup chopped nuts (optional)

Lightly butter wax paper in a 13x9x2-inch baking pan. Set aside.

In a 3-quart saucepan, combine the sugar, corn syrup, water, and salt. Cover and bring to a boil. Remove the lid and cook, stirring occasionally, to hard ball stage (260°F), or until a small amount of mixture is dropped into cold water and forms a ball that holds its shape but is pliable.

Meanwhile, in a large mixing bowl, beat the egg whites until stiff. Gradually pour the hot syrup in a small stream into the egg whites, while continuing to beat (you may need a helper for this). Add the vanilla and continue beating until the mixture holds its shape when dropped from a spoon. Fold in the nuts, if desired.

Pour into the prepared pan and cool for several hours. Invert pan and peel off wax paper. Cut into squares.

NEVER-FAIL DIVINITY

Lori Dunn

Butterscotch Fudge

Fudge of all kinds is a holiday favorite. The key to candy making is a candy thermometer; invest in a good one, and you'll always be prepared. This fudge is packed with morsels of marshamallows, nuts, and chips. A delicious caramel flavor pervades and delivers truly comforting flavors and textures.

MAKES 2 POUNDS

1 package (10 ounces) miniature marshmallows

1 package (12 ounces) butterscotch chips

2 cups chopped walnuts

4½ cups granulated sugar

1 can evaporated milk

2 sticks butter

1 tablespoon vanilla

In a large bowl, combine marshmallows, butterscotch chips, and nuts; set aside. Grease a 15½x10½x-inch baking pan and set aside.

In a large saucepan, heat sugar, milk, and butter to boiling; stir while boiling until the mixture reaches soft ball stage (235°F) on a candy thermometer. Remove from heat and stir in vanilla.

Pour hot mixture over the marshmallow mixture and beat by hand until morsels and marshmallows are melted. Pour into the prepared pan. Cool completely before cutting into squares.

BUTTERSCOTCH FUDGE

chas53/Fotolia

Colonial Peanut Butter Fudge

This quick and easy fudge is called colonial because no cooking is required to make it—an old-fashioned recipe for sure. Simply combine the ingredients and set it to cool. The texture will not be as smooth as cooked fudge, but it's delightful regardless. Different nut butters can be substituted, but you'll get the biggest flavor punch from peanut butter.

MAKES 2 POUNDS

4 cups confectioner's sugar

¼ teaspoon salt

1 cup creamy peanut butter

½ cup light corn syrup

1 stick butter, melted

1 tablespoon vanilla

1 cup nuts (optional)

Grease a 15½x10½-inch baking pan and set aside.

In a large bowl, combine the sugar and salt. In a separate bowl, beat the peanut butter, corn syrup, melted butter, and vanilla until smooth. Combine the two bowls and beat until smooth. Stir in the nuts if desired.

Pour into the prepared pan. Refrigerate to set. Cut into squares.

COLONIAL PEANUT
BUTTER FUDGE

dreambigphotos/Fotolia

Rocky Road Fudge

This is a signature fudge, indeed. It's hard to find anyone who doesn't love this classic combination. For a more intense chocolate flavor, try substituting bittersweet chocolate chips for semisweet, and use coffee extract in place of the vanilla.

MAKES 2 POUNDS

1½ cups granulated sugar

1 can (5 ounces) evaporated milk

2 tablespoons butter

¼ teaspoon salt

2 cups miniature marshmallows

1½ cups semisweet chocolate chips

½ cup chopped pecans or walnuts (optional)

1 teaspoon vanilla extract

Line an 8-inch square baking pan with a large sheet of foil, allowing excess to overlap two sides of the pan.

In a medium, heavy-duty saucepan, combine the sugar, evaporated milk, butter, and salt. Bring to full rolling boil over medium heat, stirring constantly. Boil, stirring constantly, for 4 to 5 minutes. Remove from heat.

Add marshmallows, chocolate chips, nuts, and vanilla extract. Stir vigorously for 1 minute, until marshmallows are melted.

Pour into the prepared baking pan and refrigerate for 2 hours, until firm. Hold overlapping foil and lift the fudge from the pan; remove foil. Cut into 48 bite-size pieces.

Aunt Fritz and her fudge

My very first memory of Aunt Fritz and her fudge was when I was about 3 or 4 years old. This was during World War II.

At the start of WWII, my mother's brothers volunteered to serve in the Navy. Aunt Fritz, my other aunts, and my mom would make up care packages to send to all the men.

Aunt Fritz always made candy to send, and she would let us little ones help her pick out the pecans to go in the fudge. I kept begging to help cook the fudge so one day she pulled a chair up to the stove and said, "Come on." I thought I was grown. Of course, Aunt Fritz did all the cooking, but she did allow me to help her stir the fudge. And I got to watch it being made. For a child that is a marvelous experience.

Aunt Fritz's Old-Fashioned Fudge
2 cups pure sugar
1 tablespoon cocoa
¾ cup sweet milk (do not use low/nonfat)
Pinch of salt
1 tablespoon butter
1 teaspoon vanilla
1 cup chopped pecans or walnuts, optional

Mix together sugar, cocoa, milk, and salt. Cook until it makes a ball in cold water (5 minutes or a little longer).

Add butter and vanilla. Put pan in cold water and beat until mixture starts to get thick.

Add pecans and beat together. Pour in greased pan.

For peanut butter fudge, use peanut butter instead of real butter.

Note: Aunt Fritz does not use a regulation tablespoon; she uses a large serving spoon.

Jeannie Box
via Facebook

Chapter 9
Desserts

BACK IN THE DAY, farm desserts meant not just comfort, but fuel. Threshing bees, barn-raising crews, and hay crews required tons—almost literally—of hearty noontime fare. Sure, the roast beef and potatoes were crucial, but so were the cakes, custards, and pies that topped it all off and kept the workers motivated. Mom's peach pie was so important that even when the crew was haying on the home place, her sole responsibility was to provide enough of that delightful pastry to be sure all hands got a generous helping. All over the country, women would put everything they had into the Independence Day pie contest, school bake sale, or the cakewalk at the church festival.

Husbands of good cooks were the object of considerable envy among peers. Grandpa was famous for not sharing the slice of black cherry or buffalo berry pie he pulled out of his lunch pail during the afternoon break at the foundry. His friends and coworkers had to settle for the chance to win pie at the next cakewalk.

This is the spirit of true comfort food desserts. There's no fancy culinary technique involved, but the end result is pure and delicious. In this collection—handpicked from the *Grit* archives—you'll find classic desserts like pound cake, angel food cake, and chocolate layer cake; practical, seasonal favorites like rhubarb streusel cake and plum kuchen; and family heirloom recipes like Grandma Dobbs' Old-Fashioned Date Cake and Grandma Wilson's Apple Pie.

Original Pound Cake

The creator of the pound cake must've had a large family, since the definition of a true pound cake is one made with a pound of each of the four main ingredients: butter, sugar, eggs, and flour. A large cake indeed, but perfect for a big family gathering. The versatility of a pound cake makes it indispensible; depending on your taste, add nuts, raisins, cocoa, or vanilla for flavor variations. Dust it with traditional powdered sugar, or drizzle on a simple icing (recipe below); in summer, serve it with fresh berries and sprigs of mint.

SERVES 15 TO 20

ORIGINAL POUND CAKE

iStockphoto.com/MSPhotographic

Cake:

1 pound butter
(not margarine)

1 pound sugar (2 cups)

1 pound eggs (12 large)

1 pound all-purpose flour
(4 cups before sifting)

¼ teaspoon salt

¼ cup lemon juice

1 tablespoon grated lemon rind

Icing:

1 tablespoon butter

1 box confectioner's sugar

Juice of 2 lemons

Grated rind of 1 lemon

Cream

For the cake: Heat the oven to 325°F. Grease and flour two loaf pans or one bundt pan.

Cream together butter and sugar. Add eggs, one at a time, beating after each addition.

Add flour, a little at a time. Add salt, lemon juice, and rind.

Pour into prepared pan(s). Bake for 90 minutes, until a toothpick inserted in the center comes out clean.

To make the icing: Cream together the butter, confectioner's sugar, lemon juice, and rind. To reach desired consistency, add a few teaspoons of cream.

Angel Food Cake

Springtime on the farm always brings back memories of angel food cake. With all the hens starting to lay eggs again, any recipe that calls for a dozen eggs is prized. (Make mayonnaise, custard, or eggnog with the yolks.) Use a smooth-sided tube pan for angel food cake; the center tube gives the cake batter a surface to climb on all sides, allowing it to rise higher. Grandma always cooled the cake upside down on a bottle to prevent it from falling in on itself. Frost the cake with a simple vanilla, lemon, or chocolate glaze, or serve with whipped cream and fresh berries.

SERVES 10 TO 12

12 egg whites, room temperature

1½ teaspoons cream of tartar

¾ cup granulated sugar

1½ teaspoons vanilla

½ teaspoon almond extract (optional)

1¼ cups confectioner's sugar

1 cup sifted cake flour

¼ teaspoon salt

Heat the oven to 375°F.

In a mixer bowl, beat the egg whites and cream of tartar with the whisk attachment on low speed until frothy. Increase speed to medium until foam starts to form billowy mounds. Beating constantly, add granulated sugar, 1 tablespoon at a time, beating after each addition until sugar is dissolved before adding the next. (Rub a bit of the mixture between your thumb and forefinger; it should feel completely smooth.) Continue beating until whites are glossy and stand in soft peaks. Beat in the vanilla and almond extract, if desired.

Sift confectioner's sugar, flour, and salt together twice. Sift about ½ cup of the flour mixture over the egg whites. Fold gently just until the flour disappears. Do not stir. Repeat sifting and folding in the flour mixture ½ cup at a time.

Pour the batter into an ungreased 10x4-inch tube pan. Gently cut through the batter with a metal spatula or knife to release any air pockets. Bake in the center of the oven for 30 to 40 minutes, or until the top springs back when lightly tapped with your finger. Invert the cake in the pan, with the tube resting on a bottle. Cool completely, about 2 hours. To release the cake, run a knife around the edge of the pan, being careful not to damage the crust. Cut with a serrated knife to serve.

A first attempt at cake

My mom was ill, and I was about 8 years old. I had two younger brothers and one younger sister. I stirred everything I needed into a bowl, poured the batter into Mama's black iron skillet, and put it into the oven. We had a wood range, so I put lots of wood in. (I had to stand on a wooden soda crate turned upside down.) It was pretty heavy when I lifted it out, so only made it to a stool. When Mama got up from her nap, there we all were, on our knees with spoons dipping into a crusty, clingy mess. (I had not put in any leavening or flavoring.) My parents bragged on my first cake and my siblings ate it, so I have never stopped baking.

Jackie Edson-Runyan
via Facebook

Banana Sour Cream Cake

We all understand that necessity is the mother of invention, so when you discover a bunch of overripe bananas, turn them into dessert. Banana quick bread is a favorite staple. Sour cream is a key ingredient because it adds moisture and flavor. Philip Moschitta of Chincoteague, Virginia, remembers a moist banana cake his mother used to bake in a bundt pan. Carole Shafer of Baroda, Michigan, responded with this recipe. She says, "This is the only recipe I use for the occasional indulgent treat."

SERVES 10 TO 12

3 cups sifted all-purpose flour

3 cups sugar

¼ teaspoon baking soda

2 sticks butter, softened and cut into pats

1 tablespoon lard

6 eggs

1 cup sour cream

¼ teaspoon vanilla

¼ teaspoon lemon extract

¼ teaspoon almond extract

1 cup mashed very ripe bananas (about 3 medium)

Nuts (optional)

Heat the oven to 325°F. Grease and flour a 10-inch bundt pan or two 9x5-inch loaf pans; set aside.

Combine flour, sugar, and baking soda; beat in the butter until the mixture is crumbly. Add lard or shortening, eggs, and sour cream; beat for 5 minutes. Add extracts and bananas; continue to beat for several more minutes. Add nuts, if desired.

Fill the prepared pan(s) about ¾ full. Bake for about 90 minutes, or until a toothpick inserted in the center comes out clean.

Cool the cake on a wire rack for 5 minutes, then unmold from the pan.

BANANA SOUR CREAM CAKE

Lori Dunn

This cake freezes nicely; cut into individual slices, wrap well in plastic wrap, then put into freezer bag.

Grandma Dobbs' Old-Fashioned Cake

The Christmas holiday season lends itself to all sorts of decadent sweets, like this special cake, resplendent with dates and black walnuts. Soak the dates in baking soda water to soften the skins and tenderize the fruit. Top the cake with a simple glaze.

SERVES 8 TO 10

GRANDMA DOBBS'
OLD-FASHIONED CAKE

Lori Dunn

1 teaspoon baking soda

1 cup chopped dates

1 cup boiling water

1 cup sugar

2 tablespoons lard

1 egg, beaten

2 cups all-purpose flour

1 teaspoon baking powder

1 cup chopped black walnuts

In a bowl, combine the baking soda and chopped dates.

Pour the boiling water over the dates; set aside until cool.

Heat the oven to 350°F.

To the dates, add the sugar, lard or shortening, egg, flour, and baking powder. Mix well. Stir in the black walnuts.

Bake in a 10-inch cast iron skillet for 40 to 45 minutes until a toothpick inserted in the middle comes out clean.

Watch the salt

When I was baking for the first time around the age of 11, I wanted to surprise my parents with homemade chocolate cupcakes. I didn't know the difference between tablespoon and teaspoon. You guessed it—a tablespoon of salt doesn't taste very good. Our dog, who would eat sour pickles, wouldn't touch them, nor would the pigs we owned eat them. Thirty years later we still laugh at it. I now make sure my children can tell the difference.

Rosa Gandyra-Mooney
via Facebook

Chocolate Layer Cake with Mocha Cream Frosting

This go-to chocolate layer cake is a classic for birthdays and anniversaries. The coffee in the mocha cream frosting intensifies the chocolate flavor. Decorate the top with sprinkles, jimmies, nonpareils, gumdrops, chocolate chips—the sky's the limit.

CHOCOLATE LAYER CAKE WITH
MOCHA CREAM FROSTING
iStockphoto.com/Funwithfood

Cake:

2 cups sugar

1¾ cups unsifted all-purpose flour

¾ cup cocoa

1½ teaspoons baking soda

¾ teaspoon salt

1⅔ cups milk

½ cup butter

3 eggs

1 teaspoon vanilla extract

Frosting:

2⅔ cups confectioner's sugar

¼ cup cocoa

6 tablespoons butter

2 tablespoons strong coffee

2 to 3 tablespoons milk

1 teaspoon vanilla extract

Heat oven to 350°F. Grease and flour two 9-inch layer pans or one 13x9x2-inch baking pan; set aside.

In a large mixing bowl, combine sugar, flour, cocoa, baking soda, and salt. Add the milk, butter, eggs, and vanilla. Blend ingredients, using electric mixer on low speed, for 30 seconds. Beat on medium speed for 3 minutes.

Pour evenly into prepared pans. Bake for 30 to 35 minutes for layers; 35 to 40 minutes for a single pan, until a toothpick inserted into the center comes out clean. Cool in pans on a wire rack for 15 to 20 minutes.

Run a knife around the edge of the pan to loosen. Invert the cakes onto a lightly greased wire rack to continue cooling. Cool completely before frosting.

To make frosting: in a bowl, whisk together the confectioner's sugar and cocoa.

In a large bowl, cream the butter with ½ cup of the sugar-cocoa mixture. Add the remaining sugar mixture alternatively with the coffee and milk, beating until a spreading consistency is reached. Blend in vanilla.

Place one layer of the cake on a plate or cake stand. Frost on all sides. Top with the second layer and finish frosting.

Grandma Wilson's Apple Pie

Grandma Wilson was an inventive country cook who never missed an opportunity to add something special to her recipes. To the American country classic, apple pie, she added a custardy filling of cream and egg yolks. Be sure to use a tart, firm apple, like Granny Smith or Pippin.

SERVES 8 TO 10

GRANDMA WILSON'S
APPLE PIE

iStockphoto.com/arihen

1 cup sugar

2 tablespoons all-purpose flour

½ teaspoon ground cinnamon

6 cups pared and chopped apples (about 6 medium apples)

1 9-inch deep-dish pie crust, unbaked

2 tablespoons butter

1 cup heavy whipping cream

4 egg yolks

Heat oven to 375°F.

In a large bowl, combine sugar, flour, and cinnamon; add the apples and toss gently to coat. Spoon into the pastry shell, mounding to center. Dot with butter.

Bake for 30 minutes, or until the crust begins to brown and the apples are tender. Remove from the oven and reduce the oven temperature to 325°F.

In a 2-cup measuring cup, beat the whipping cream and egg yolks. Pour over the apple filling, pressing lightly with a fork so that the mixture seeps into the filling. Return to the oven and continue baking for an additional 30 minutes, or until the crust is golden and the filling is bubbly. Cool to room temperature before serving. Refrigerate leftovers.

Old-Fashioned Sugar Cream Pie

This old-timey pie reflects the simple ingredients of the past. With just a few pantry staples and farm-fresh milk and cream, Mom could have a proper dessert on the table. This pie goes by many different names, but our favorite is chess pie. How did it get that name? In the southern United States, when tourists ask, "What kind of pie is this?" the locals respond in a breathy southern drawl, "It's chess (just) pie."

SERVES 8 TO 10

½ cup sugar

½ cup brown sugar

¼ teaspoon salt

2 tablespoons all-purpose flour

1 cup half-and-half or milk

1 cup whipping cream

2 tablespoons butter

1 unbaked pie shell

Heat oven to 425°F.

In a small bowl, mix together the sugars, salt, and flour.

In a saucepan, heat the half-and-half, whipping cream, and butter until warm. Transfer to a large bowl and add the dry ingredients.

Pour the mixture into the pie shell. Bake for 15 minutes; reduce oven temperature to 350°F and bake for an additional 30 minutes. Cool thoroughly on a wire rack before slicing.

OLD-FASHIONED SUGAR CREAM PIE

Lori Dunn

Homemade pie crust and cinnamon treats

I can remember my mom making homemade pie crust. With the dough that was left over (she made extra), she would make strips and brush butter on them and sprinkle with cinnamon and sugar for our treats after school. We could smell the aroma of them the closer we got home. We were blessed with our mama.

Glenda Lewis-Pennel
via Facebook

Rhubarb Streusel Pie

Rhubarb is often the first edible to be harvested from the garden, its neon-green stalks emerging through the last of the snow. This vegetable-that's-used-as-a-fruit is extremely tart and always needs its sour nature tamed with sugar or strawberries. To further mellow the tartness of rhubarb, soak it in a gallon of cold water for 20 minutes before you chop it.

SERVES 8

Streusel:

⅓ cup all-purpose flour

½ cup sugar

2 tablespoons melted butter

Pie:

1 9-inch pie crust

½ cup sugar

½ cup all-purpose flour

3 cups chopped rhubarb (12 to 14 ounces)

1 can (14 ounces) sweetened condensed milk

Heat oven to 425°F.

For the streusel: Combine the flour and sugar. Stir in the melted butter until a coarse meal forms. Set aside.

For the pie: Line 9-inch pie plate with pie dough.

Combine sugar and flour. Sprinkle about ⅓ of the mixture on the dough. Lay in the rhubarb. Sprinkle with the remaining flour and sugar mixture. Pour sweetened condensed milk over all.

Top with the streusel. Bake for 30 to 40 minutes, or until well-browned and bubbly. Serve with ice cream or whipped cream.

RHUBARB STREUSEL PIE

iStockphoto.com/Innershadows

Apple Crisp

Fall means the arrival of fresh apples and the opening of you-pick orchards all over the country. After a day of cider drinking and apple picking, toss together this super simple apple crisp for dessert—no need to peel the apples. Top each bowl with a scoop of vanilla or cinnamon ice cream.

SERVES 6

APPLE CRISP

Karen K. Will

4 cups apples, sliced

¼ cup water

1 teaspoon cinnamon

¼ teaspoon nutmeg

½ teaspoon salt

1 cup sugar

¾ cup unbleached all-purpose flour

⅓ cup butter, cubed

Heat the oven to 350°F.

Place the apples in a deep-dish pie plate. Sprinkle the water over the apples. Sprinkle on the cinnamon, nutmeg, and salt.

In a large bowl, use a pastry blender to mix the sugar, flour, and butter. Pour the mixture evenly over the apples.

Bake uncovered for 40 minutes, until bubbling. Allow to cool for 15 minutes before serving.

Grinding apples for candy

I remember being little, age 6 or so, and my mom giving my brother and me a quarter to sit on the kitchen table and turn the food mill for making applesauce. We'd sit up there so excited and eager to help out because when all the applesauce was made and canned, she'd take us to the local smoke shop (two towns over) and let us spend our hard-earned money on penny candy. Twenty-five pieces of candy was a big deal to us back then. We'd leave the store skipping wearing our biggest smiles with a little brown bag in hand filled with our tasty treasures. Life was wonderful.

Catrina Mooney Kingsley
via Facebook

Skillet Peach Cobbler

Make peach cobbler when local farm stands are overflowing with juicy peaches. This unfussy, one-skillet recipe suits the harried days of summer. To get the fuzzy skins off the peaches, blanch them in simmering water for 15 seconds, then transfer to a waiting bowl of ice water. The skins should slip off nicely. Serve with Homemade Whipped Cream (page 195) or ice cream.

SERVES 8

Filling:

1 stick butter (½ cup)

4 cups peeled and sliced fresh peaches

½ cup brown sugar

½ cup granulated sugar

1 teaspoon cinnamon

1 cup heavy cream

Topping:

1 cup unbleached all-purpose flour

2 teaspoons baking powder

¼ teaspoon salt

4 tablespoons salted butter, cold and cut into chunks

¼ cup plus 1 tablespoon turbinado sugar, divided

⅓ cup half-and-half

SKILLET PEACH COBBLER

Karen K. Will

Heat the oven to 350°F.

To make cobbler, melt the butter in a large (12-inch) cast-iron skillet. Add peaches, sugars, cinnamon, and cream. Bring to a boil, then reduce heat and simmer, uncovered, for 20 minutes, stirring throughout.

While peaches are cooking, make the topping. In a large bowl, combine the flour, baking powder, and salt. Using a pastry blender, cut in the butter until the mixture resembles coarse crumbs. Add ¼ cup sugar and blend well. Gradually mix in the half-and-half until the dough just comes together.

Spoon the topping over the peach mixture in the skillet. Sprinkle the remaining tablespoon of sugar on top.

Bake uncovered for 40 minutes until bubbling. Allow to cool for 15 minutes before serving.

Plum Kuchen

For kids raised on the farm, that first bite of a ripe plum in July brings with it a flood of childhood memories: searching every plum thicket within a 5-mile radius for enough fruit for Mom to make jelly. If not jelly, then some delicious summery dessert like this kuchen. Serve with a dollop of old-fashioned vanilla ice cream.

SERVES 8 TO 10

2 cups all-purpose flour

3 teaspoons baking powder

½ teaspoon salt

1 cup sugar, divided

8 tablespoons (1 stick) butter, divided

1 egg

¾ cup milk

4 cups seeded and quartered plums (approximately 2 pounds)

1 teaspoon cinnamon

½ teaspoon nutmeg

Whipped cream or vanilla ice cream (optional)

PLUM KUCHEN

Fotolia/farbkombinat

Heat the oven to 400°F. Grease a 13x9x2-inch baking pan; set aside.

In a mixing bowl, combine the flour, baking powder, salt, and ¼ cup sugar. Cut in 6 tablespoons butter; blend until crumbly.

In another bowl, beat together the egg and milk; stir into flour mixture. Blend well.

Pour batter into the prepared pan. Arrange plum quarters, overlapping, on top. Melt the remaining 2 tablespoons butter and drizzle over the plums.

Mix the remaining ¾ cup sugar with the cinnamon and nutmeg; sprinkle over the plums.

Bake for 40 minutes.

Cool for at least 30 minutes before serving.

Strawberry Rhubarb Crisp

Crisps are the easiest, most rustic type of dessert to prepare. Not fussy or complicated, a crisp can be improvised with all kinds of substitutions—brown sugar for white, wheat flour for white, chopped nuts for the oats. Rhubarb's sour and tart flavor is often mellowed with the sweetness of strawberries, as in this recipe, but you could even substitute with another sweet fruit, like plums or peaches. Just use what you have and enjoy.

SERVES 9

Filling:

1 cup white sugar

3 tablespoons all-purpose flour

3 cups sliced fresh strawberries (about 1 pound)

3 cups rhubarb, diced (about 5 stalks or 1 pound)

Topping:

¾ cup all-purpose flour

½ cup packed brown sugar

½ cup rolled oats

½ cup butter, cut into small chunks

Heat the oven to 375°F. In a large bowl, mix the white sugar, 3 tablespoons of flour, strawberries, and rhubarb. Let it sit for a few minutes to draw out the juices, and then mix well again. Pour into an 8x8-inch baking dish.

To make the topping, put the remaining ingredients into the bowl of a food processor. Pulse 4 or 5 times, until the mixture is crumbly. Pour the crumbly mixture on top of the fruit, and spread it out evenly. Bake for 45 minutes, or until crispy and golden.

Pumpkin Custard

The trick to making a custard is not cooking the eggs. Hot liquid is gradually added to the beaten eggs to temper them; don't rush this step, or you'll end up with scrambled eggs.

1 cup milk

1 package (8 ounces) cream cheese, softened

½ cup brown sugar

¼ cup honey

2 eggs

1 cup pumpkin purée

1 teaspoon vanilla

1 teaspoon allspice

1 teaspoon cinnamon

Whipped cream (optional)

Heat the oven to 350°F. Grease six ramekins or custard cups; set aside.

In a saucepan, combine the milk, cream cheese, brown sugar, and honey. Cook slowly over low heat, stirring constantly until honey is dissolved, taking care not to scald or curdle the mixture.

In a small glass bowl, beat the eggs. Add a spoonful of the heated mixture to the eggs and mix; add another spoonful and mix. Pour the egg mixture into the saucepan with the milk mixture and then remove it from heat. Stir in the pumpkin, vanilla, allspice, and cinnamon.

Pour the mixture evenly into the ramekins, filling about ¾ full. Place the ramekins in a larger baking dish with 1 inch of water, and bake for 1 hour and 15 minutes, or until a knife inserted in the center comes out clean.

Serve warm or chilled, topped with sweetened whipped cream, if desired.

Homemade Whipped Cream

You and your fellow eaters will surely appreciate a dollop of homemade pure whipped cream on your warm cobbler or crisp. To whip by hand, it will take about 5 to 10 minutes; get your kids or spouse to take a turn at the whisk. Homemade whipped cream whips easier and faster when you use nonhomogenized, nonultrapasteurized cream.

MAKES 1 CUP

1 cup heavy whipping cream

2 tablespoons sugar

1 teaspoon vanilla extract

Place 1 cup of heavy cream in a large mixing bowl.

Add sugar and beat by hand or with an electric mixer on low speed for 30 seconds.

Add vanilla and beat on high speed until soft peaks form.

Cranking out the homemade ice cream

I remember the summers of my youth spent camping in the big pine forests of Northern California with hoards of my extended family. My great-uncle Bert and his wife, Jackie, were our camp ambassadors, holding court from their circa 1950s Airstream trailer. Aunt Jackie would call us kids round to help make ice cream. Ice was procured from the closest mini mart, and we'd all take turns cranking the old-fashioned churn, complete with rock salt. Peaches were always in season and how we all looked forward to homemade peach ice cream after our supper of rainbow trout, cooked over a campfire. Those were really the days.

Karen K. Will
Scranton, Kansas

Creamy Rice Pudding

This classic rice pudding is just like the kind Grandma used to make—creamy and comforting in its simplicity. Start this early in the day and get it chilled before dessert time. Serve plain or with cinnamon and sugar, shaved maple sugar, or Homemade Whipped Cream.

SERVES 6

½ cup rice

2 cups evaporated milk

2 cups hot water

¼ teaspoon nutmeg

½ teaspoon salt

Rinse the rice in a colander. Combine the rice with remaining ingredients in the top of a double boiler. Cover and cook over boiling water for 2 hours.

Allow pudding to cool for 30 minutes. Transfer to a container and chill for several hours in the refrigerator before serving.

Peach Ice Cream

Nothing says summer like the arrival of the first luscious peaches of the season. When summer gives you peaches, make ice cream. For the best ice cream, select the most fabulously fragrant, perfectly ripe peaches available. Adding just a touch of cinnamon accents the peachy flavor without giving the ice cream a pronounced cinnamon flavor.

MAKES 5 CUPS

1½ cups peeled and sliced very ripe yellow peaches

1 tablespoon freshly squeezed lemon juice

⅔ cup sugar, divided

3 large egg yolks

⅛ teaspoon salt

¾ cup hot milk

½ cup cold milk

¼ teaspoon cinnamon

1½ teaspoons vanilla extract

1¼ cups heavy whipping cream

PEACH ICE CREAM

iStockphoto.com/TheCrimsonMonkey

In a medium bowl (or a 2-quart glass measuring cup to make pouring into the machine easier), stir together the sliced peaches, lemon juice, and half the sugar; let this stand at room temperature for 1 hour to macerate.

In the bottom pan of a double boiler, heat 1 inch of water to a gentle simmer. In the top pan of the double boiler, whisk together the egg yolks, salt, and remaining sugar until well blended.

Gradually whisk in the hot milk and cook over hot—not boiling—water, stirring constantly, until the mixture thickens and registers between 160°F and 170°F; do not boil. Stir in cold milk.

With a potato masher, pastry blender, or fork, mash the macerated peaches until slightly chunky or completely smooth, whichever you prefer. Use a blender or food processor for a supersmooth puree. Stir in the cinnamon.

Add the custard to the peaches, then whisk in the vanilla and cream. Cover and refrigerate until well chilled, at least 4 hours or overnight.

Churn in an ice cream maker according to manufacturer's instructions. Transfer the soft ice cream to a freezer-safe, airtight container and place in the freezer for at least 4 hours.

Simple Butter Pecan Ice Cream

You will be hard-pressed to find a soul who doesn't love butter pecan ice cream, and if it's homemade, consider the task impossible. Whether you use an old-fashioned hand-cranked churn with ice and rock salt or one of the modern prechilled canister models, you'll appreciate the pure taste of this nutty, buttery, from-scratch ice cream because it was made with your own elbow grease.

MAKES 5 CUPS

⅓ **cup sugar**

⅓ **packed cup dark brown sugar**

2 teaspoons vanilla extract

Pinch salt

1 cup milk, whole or reduced fat

2 cups heavy whipping cream

2 tablespoons unsalted butter

1 cup finely chopped pecans (4 ounces)

⅛ **teaspoon salt**

In a medium bowl (or use a 2-quart glass measure cup to make pouring into the machine easier), whisk together the sugars, vanilla, salt, and milk until the sugars are dissolved. Stir in heavy cream. Cover and refrigerate for at least 4 hours or overnight.

At least 1 hour before making ice cream, melt butter in small skillet over medium-low heat. Add pecans and salt, and cook, stirring frequently, until the pecans are toasted, about 6 to 8 minutes. Set aside to cool completely.

Churn cream mixture in an ice cream maker according to manufacturer's instructions. Mix until thickened, about 10 to 15 minutes. With machine still running, pour toasted pecans through the spout and let mix in completely, up to 5 minutes.

Transfer soft ice cream to a freezer-safe airtight container and place in the freezer for at least 4 hours. Remove from the freezer 15 minutes before serving.

SIMPLE BUTTER PECAN
ICE CREAM

Lori Dunn

Plum Dumplings

Farm families are known for their passels of kids, so it's great to have recipes that kids can help with. This dessert is perfect for those occasions, requiring only the rolling out and pinching of dough. Pam Coloton of Buchanan, Virginia, sent us this recipe that looks fun as well as delicious.

SERVES 5

PLUM DUMPLINGS

iStockphoto/rista2402

Plain pastry for a double-crust pie

10 blue plums, washed and dried

Scant ½ cup sugar, divided

Water or egg white

Cinnamon (optional)

Cream (optional)

Heat the oven to 425°F.

Roll out the pastry to a rectangular shape, about ⅛ inch thick. Cut into 4-inch squares.

Place a whole plum in the center of each square and sprinkle with 2 teaspoons sugar. Wet the edges of the crust with water or egg white. Bring the corners up to the center and pinch the edges together firmly. Place dumplings on a baking sheet, about 2 inches apart.

Bake for 25 to 30 minutes.

Combine cinnamon and remaining sugar. To eat, cut dumplings in half, remove the pits, and top with a little cinnamon-sugar and cream, if desired.

Chocolate Soufflé

A classic chocolate soufflé is pure comfort—so simple, so decadent. Follow this age-old rule: the soufflé doesn't wait for the guests, the guests wait for the soufflé. Be ready to whisk the soufflé to the table as soon as it's out of the oven. Serve by gently breaking the top crust into portions with two forks held back-to-back. Then lightly spoon the soufflé onto plates, including some center and some crust in each serving.

To make a mocha-flavored soufflé, dissolve 1 tablespoon of instant coffee or espresso powder in 1 tablespoon of hot water; add this when adding the vanilla to the chocolate mixture.

SERVES 8

½ **cup sugar, divided**

⅓ **cup unsweetened cocoa powder**

¼ **cup all-purpose flour**

⅛ **teaspoon salt**

1 **cup milk**

½ **teaspoon vanilla**

4 **eggs, separated, room temperature**

½ **teaspoon cream of tartar**

CHOCOLATE SOUFFLÉ

American Egg Board

Heat the oven to 350°F.

In a medium saucepan, mix ¼ cup sugar with cocoa powder, flour, and salt; gradually whisk in the milk until smooth. Cook over medium heat, stirring constantly, until the mixture thickens and boils. Stir in the vanilla. Remove from heat.

In a mixer bowl using the whisk attachment, beat the egg whites and cream of tartar on high speed until foamy. Beating constantly, add the remaining ¼ cup sugar, 2 tablespoons at a time, beating after each addition until the sugar is dissolved. (Rub a bit of mixture between thumb and forefinger; it should feel completely smooth.) Continue beating until the egg whites are glossy and stand in soft peaks.

Stir the egg yolks into the warm cocoa sauce until blended. Gently but thoroughly fold the yolk mixture into whites until no streaks of white remain.

Carefully pour the batter into an ungreased 1½- to 2-quart soufflé dish. Bake until soufflé is puffy, delicately browned, and shakes slightly when oven rack is moved gently back and forth, 30 to 40 minutes. Serve immediately.

Note: Dust soufflé with confectioner's sugar and serve with whipped cream.

Strawberry Shortcake with Herbs and Whipped Cream

A perfectly executed strawberry shortcake is hard to come by; but a delightfully crumbly biscuit cake at the base, with tiny ripe, sweet strawberries tumbling about, is as good as it gets. Early summer means not only those tiny, sweet strawberries everywhere, but an abundant herb garden at its peak. Why not pair the two? The grenadine is an unexpected yet inspired syrup for strawberries.

MAKES ABOUT 8 3-INCH SHORTCAKES

Topping:

About 5 sprigs lemon balm or orange mint (optional)

1 pint whipping cream

1 quart strawberries, rinsed, hulled, and sliced

2 to 3 tablespoons grenadine syrup

Handful sweet woodruff sprigs, optional

1 heaping tablespoon sugar

Shortcakes:

2 cups unbleached all-purpose flour

3 teaspoons baking powder

Scant ½ teaspoon salt

3 tablespoons sugar, divided

6 tablespoons unsalted butter

1 cup half-and-half or whole milk

2 tablespoons finely chopped orange mint or lemon balm, optional

1 tablespoon unsalted butter, melted

To make topping: Bruise the herb sprigs and place in a bowl with whipping cream; cover and refrigerate. In another bowl, toss the berries with the grenadine and woodruff and stir to mix. Let stand for at least 30 minutes, or up to a few hours.

Heat the oven to 400°F. Lightly butter a baking sheet; set aside.

In a bowl or food processor, combine the flour, baking powder, salt, and 2 tablespoons sugar. Cut in the butter until it becomes a coarse meal. Add the half-and-half to the dry ingredients and mix until just blended. Add the chopped herbs and toss; don't over mix.

Turn the dough onto a floured surface and knead 8 to 10 times. Roll or pat the dough to about ¾ inch thick. Using a 3-inch biscuit cutter, cut out rounds, using all the dough. Gather up scraps, knead together, roll out, and cut again. Place the rounds of dough on a baking sheet, brush the tops with melted butter, and sprinkle with 1 tablespoon sugar.

Bake in the center of the oven for about 15 minutes, or until golden brown. Cool the shortcakes on a wire rack for at least 5 minutes before splitting open; they are best served warm, but room temperature is fine.

While cakes are baking, remove the herb sprigs from the whipping cream, add a heaping tablespoon of sugar and whisk until softly whipped.

To assemble shortcakes, split them in half. Place a spoonful of berries on bottom half with a bit of juice. Add a dollop of whipped cream and set the top half. Repeat with fruit and cream and garnish the top with a berry slice and an edible flower. Serve immediately.

STRAWBERRY SHORTCAKE
iStockphoto.com/Diane Diederich

Chapter 10
Jams, Jellies, and Preserves

IF THERE IS ANYTHING that reminds us of generations past, it's the memory of canning season in the kitchen. Bushel baskets overflowed with fresh apples and peaches; aprons filled with ripe blackberries or gooseberries plucked from thickets; gallons of tomatoes or peppers needed preserving. When canning time came, all members of the family were drafted into service, each with a specific task. Such memories certainly can't be bought, but only made by hand.

Jams, jellies, and preserves make the ultimate pantry staples and gifts. But what's the difference among these soft spreads? Jam is made from cooking fruit pulp or crushed fruit until it rounds up on a spoon; jam is firm but spreadable.

Jelly is made from cooking fruit juice, strained from whole fruit; clear and gelatinous, jelly holds its shape yet is easily spreadable. Preserves are made by cooking larger chunks of fruit with sugar; tender and plump, preserves do not hold their shape when spooned from the jar. Fruit butter results from slow cooking pulp and sugar into a thick spread—thick enough to mound on a spoon.

When making these soft spreads, use top-quality fruit—some underripe for extra pectin and acid, some perfectly ripe for best flavor. Always wash the fruit thoroughly and follow recipe instructions to the letter. Canning recipes cannot handle substitutions or omissions.

How to Process Jams and Jellies

If you are new to canning, please review a current copy of the *Ball Blue Book of Preserving*, which will tell you everything you need to know about the process. Here is a summary of how to process jams and jellies:

1. Wash jars and screw bands in hot, soapy water, then rinse with warm water; jars can also be washed in the dishwasher using a full cycle. Drain bands and jars before filling.Place flat lids in a saucepan and cover with water; bring water to simmer (180°F) for 10 minutes. Leave the lids in hot water until ready to use, removing them one at a time as needed.
2. Bring a boiling-water canner, half-full with water, to simmer (180°F).
3. Ladle hot jelly mixture quickly into the prepared jars, leaving ¼ inch headspace. Remove air bubbles by placing a nonmetallic spatula inside the jar and moving it from side to side and around the edge of the jar. Wipe jar rims and threads with a clean, damp paper towel; cover with two-piece lids, screwing bands tightly.
4. Place the jars on the elevated rack in the canner, then lower the rack into the canner. Water must cover the jars by 1 to 2 inches, so add boiling water if needed. Cover and bring water to a gentle boil. Process jellies for 5 minutes, or jams for 10 minutes. Remove jars using a jar lifter and place upright on a towel to cool completely. After jars cool, check seals by pressing middle of lid with your finger. If the lid springs back, it is not sealed and refrigeration is necessary.
5. Let the jars stand at room temperature for 24 hours. Store unopened jams and jellies in a cool, dry, dark place for up to 1 year. Refrigerate opened jams and jellies for up to 3 weeks.

Note: For altitudes above 1,000 feet, adjust processing time: 1,001 to 3,000, add 5 minutes; 3,001 to 6,000, add 10 minutes; 6,001 to 8,000, add 15 minutes; 8,001 to 10,000, add 20 minutes.

Gelling Test

Some of our recipes do not call for pectin, and in this case, you will need to test your jam or jelly for doneness before jarring. Once you think it's done, remove it from the heat.

To test gelling using the sheet test, dip a cool, metal spoon into the boiling jelly. Lift a spoonful of jelly and tip over a plate so the jelly drops off the spoon. If jelly drops off in multiple drops, it is not done. Return pan to heat and continue cooking. Test again. When jelly drops off the spoon in a solid sheet, it is done. Refer to the *Ball Blue Book of Preserving* for a visual aid for the gelling test.

Low-Sugar Sweet Cherry Jam

MAKES 5 HALF-PINTS

4 cups pitted, chopped, and mashed sweet cherries

¼ cup lemon or lime juice

4 teaspoons calcium water (included in Pomona's Pectin box)

½ to 1 cup honey or ¾ cup to 2 cups sugar

3 teaspoons Pomona's Pectin powder

LOW-SUGAR SWEET CHERRY JAM

bit24/Fotolia

Prepare fruit and measure into large saucepan with lemon or lime juice. Add calcium water to fruit (see Pomona's directions for making calcium water) and stir well.

Measure sugar or cold/room temperature honey into a separate bowl. Thoroughly mix pectin powder into sweetener.

Bring fruit to a boil. Add pectin-sweetener mixture to fruit and stir vigorously for 1 to 2 minutes while cooking to dissolve pectin. Return to boil and remove from heat.

Ladle hot jam mixture quickly into the prepared jars, leaving ¼ inch headspace. Remove air bubbles by placing a nonmetallic spatula inside the jar and moving it from side to side and around the edge of the jar. Wipe jar rims and threads with a clean, damp paper towel; cover with two-piece lids, screwing bands tightly.

Process 10 minutes in boiling-water canner: adjust for altitude if necessary.

Note: If you have sour cherries, you don't need to add the lemon/lime juice, and you only need 2 teaspoons of pectin and 2 teaspoons of calcium water for 4 cups of mashed fruit.

Optional: To soften firm fruit, bring to a boil with ½ cup of water, simmer 5 minutes, stirring occasionally.

Low-Sugar Strawberry-Rhubarb Jam

MAKES 5 HALF-PINTS

LOW-SUGAR STRAWBERRY-RHUBARB JAM

StefanieB/Fotolia

2 cups mashed strawberries

2 cups cooked rhubarb (chop rhubarb, add a little water, cook until soft, measure)

2 teaspoons calcium water (included in Pomona's Pectin box)

½ to 1 cup honey or ¾ cup to 2 cups sugar

2½ teaspoons Pomona's Pectin powder

Prepare fruit and measure into large saucepan. Add calcium water to fruit (see Pomona's directions for making calcium water) and stir well.

Measure sugar or cold/room temperature honey into a separate bowl. Thoroughly mix pectin powder into sweetener.

Bring fruit to a boil. Add pectin-sweetener mixture to fruit and stir vigorously for 1 to 2 minutes while cooking to dissolve pectin. Return to boil and remove from heat.

Ladle hot jam mixture quickly into the prepared jars, leaving ¼ inch headspace. Remove air bubbles by placing a nonmetallic spatula inside the jar and moving it from side to side and around the edge of the jar. Wipe jar rims and threads with a clean, damp paper towel; cover with two-piece lids, screwing bands tightly.

Process 10 minutes in boiling-water canner; adjust for altitude if necessary.

Saving the strawberries

I'll never forget the morning my mom roused us from bed in a panic, and I didn't know if it was a fire, tornado, or what at first. I remember it even though I wasn't yet a kindergartener, and that meant I didn't have to get ready for school. I followed my mom out the back door on a run, me not really in the know for what the problem was at this point, but I soon learned as we ran to the garden. *Frost.* And frost meant our strawberry patch could be ruined in an instant, and now it was up to Mom and me to try and save them.

On this morning, we sprayed them with water, trying to keep the frost off and warm them up, then we covered them with a tarp to capture the heat. We later harvested them, and they were fine. It's a good thing, too, since one of the best parts of Mom's canning season was homemade strawberry jam, which we not only ate year-round, but gave as gifts to neighboring farms and friends. It's the best strawberry jam I've ever had.

Caleb D. Regan
Lawrence, Kansas

Raspberry Jam

MAKES 8 TO 10 HALF-PINTS

24 ounces fresh red raspberries, chopped

3 cups water

1 box powdered pectin

7 cups sugar

In a large saucepan, stir together the raspberries, water, and pectin. Bring to a boil, stirring constantly. Continue stirring while adding sugar. Maintain hard boil while stirring constantly for 3 minutes. Remove from heat. Stir until foam is reabsorbed. (The foam contains pectin.)

Ladle hot jelly mixture quickly into the prepared jars, leaving ¼ inch headspace. Remove air bubbles by placing a nonmetallic spatula inside the jar and moving it from side to side and around the edge of the jar. Wipe jar rims and threads with a clean, damp paper towel; cover with two-piece lids, screwing bands tightly.

Process 10 minutes in a boiling-water canner; adjust for altitude if necessary.

RASPBERRY JAM

Christian Jung/Fotolia

Fig Jam

MAKES 10 TO 12 HALF-PINTS

6 cups figs, crushed and chopped

2 lemons, washed

½ cup lemon juice

1 cup water

1 box powdered pectin

8 cups sugar

Place chopped figs into a large saucepan.

Zest one lemon. Slice the second lemon (including rind) into ⅛-inch-thick slices and cut to form 8 triangles.

Add lemon zest, lemon juice, and lemon slices to figs. Stir water and pectin into fig mixture. Bring to a boil, stirring constantly.

Add sugar. Return to a rolling boil and stir constantly for 3 minutes. Remove from heat. Stir until foam is reabsorbed.

Ladle hot jam mixture quickly into the prepared jars, leaving ¼ inch headspace. Remove air bubbles by placing a nonmetallic spatula inside the jar and moving it from side to side and around the edge of the jar. Wipe jar rims and threads with a clean, damp paper towel; cover with two-piece lids, screwing bands tightly.

Process 15 minutes in boiling-water canner; adjust for altitude if necessary.

FIG JAM

Vesna Cvorovic/Fotolia

Apricot Jam

MAKES 7 TO 8 HALF-PINTS

2½ pounds fully ripe apricots, peeled and pitted

2¼ cups sugar

2¼ cup white corn syrup

1 box powdered pectin

Grind the apricots in a food mill, or crush them finely. Measure out 3½ cups and place in a 5- or 6-quart saucepan. Combine sugar and syrup in a bowl; set aside.

Heat the apricots over high heat; when the mixture is very hot, add the pectin and bring to a boil. When the mixture comes to a hard boil, add the sugar and syrup mixture all at once. Bring to a full rolling boil and boil hard for 1 minute, stirring constantly. Remove from heat. Skim foam.

Ladle hot jam mixture quickly into the prepared jars, leaving ¼ inch headspace. Remove air bubbles by placing a nonmetallic spatula inside the jar and moving it from side to side and around the edge of the jar. Wipe jar rims and threads with a clean, damp paper towel; cover with two-piece lids, screwing bands tightly.

Process 15 minutes in a boiling-water canner; adjust for altitude if necessary.

APRICOT JAM

BeTa-Artworks/Fotolia

Carrot Jam

MAKES 8 HALF-PINTS

6 cups sliced carrots

½ cup lemon juice

6½ cups sugar

1 teaspoon cinnamon

6 ounces fruit pectin

Place carrots in a large saucepan and cover with water. Cook for 15 minutes, until tender. Drain and puree in a blender.

Transfer carrots to a large saucepan and add lemon juice, sugar, and cinnamon. Bring to a boil and boil for 1 minute, then remove from heat. Add pectin and let stand for 5 minutes. Stir well once or twice.

Ladle hot jam mixture quickly into the prepared jars, leaving ¼ inch headspace. Remove air bubbles by placing a nonmetallic spatula inside the jar and moving it from side to side and around the edge of the jar. Wipe jar rims and threads with a clean, damp paper towel; cover with two-piece lids, screwing bands tightly.

Process 10 minutes in a boiling-water canner; adjust for altitude if necessary.

CARROT JAM

Vanillla/Fotolia

Honey Peach Jam

MAKES 5 HALF-PINTS

3 pounds peaches

2 cups strained honey

3 tablespoons lemon juice

1½ tablespoons whole cloves

¾ teaspoon whole allspice

3 teaspoons broken cinnamon stick

Peel, stone, and slice the peaches; drain off juice into a measuring cup. Add enough water to make ¾ cup liquid; place in a large saucepan. Add the peaches, honey, and lemon juice.

Combine the cloves, allspice, and cinnamon; tie in a cheesecloth bag. Add bag to peach mixture and boil slowly, stirring frequently, until thick and jellied. Remove from heat and remove spice bag.

Ladle hot jam mixture quickly into the prepared jars, leaving ¼ inch headspace. Remove air bubbles by placing a nonmetallic spatula inside the jar and moving it from side to side and around the edge of the jar. Wipe jar rims and threads with a clean, damp paper towel; cover with two-piece lids, screwing bands tightly.

Process 10 minutes in a boiling-water canner; adjust for altitude if necessary.

HONEY PEACH JAM

nolonely/Fotolia

Peach Jam

MAKES 7 TO 8 HALF-PINTS

PEACH JAM

zigzagmtart/Fotolia

2½ pounds firm peaches

3¾ cups sugar

3 cups white syrup

½ teaspoon almond extract (optional)

1 cup liquid pectin

Scald and peel the peaches; chop or cut very fine. Measure out 3½ cups mixture and place in a large saucepan with sugar and syrup. Mix well and bring to a full rolling boil.

Boil rapidly for 12 to 19 minutes, stirring constantly. Remove from heat; stir in almond extract and pectin. Cool mixture somewhat, alternately stirring and skimming.

Ladle hot jam mixture quickly into the prepared jars, leaving ¼ inch headspace. Remove air bubbles by placing a nonmetallic spatula inside the jar and moving it from side to side and around the edge of the jar. Wipe jar rims and threads with a clean, damp paper towel; cover with two-piece lids, screwing bands tightly.

Process 10 minutes in a boiling-water canner; adjust for altitude if necessary.

Fresh Plum Jam

MAKES 12 HALF-PINTS

4 pounds fresh plums

½ cup water

1 box (1¾ ounces) pectin

8 cups sugar

Wash the plums, remove pits, and chop the pulp. Place chopped plums in a 6-quart pot or kettle; add water and bring to a simmer. Cover and continue to simmer for 5 minutes.

Add pectin and bring to a rapid boil, stirring rapidly and constantly. Add sugar and bring to full rolling boil, stirring constantly. Boil for 1 minute.

Remove from heat. Skim off foam and continue to stir then skim after each stirring for 5 minutes, allowing mixture to cool slightly.

Ladle hot jam mixture quickly into the prepared jars, leaving ¼ inch headspace. Remove air bubbles by placing a nonmetallic spatula inside the jar and moving it from side to side and around the edge of the jar. Wipe jar rims and threads with a clean, damp paper towel; cover with two-piece lids, screwing bands tightly.

Process for 20 minutes in a boiling-water canner; adjust for altitude if necessary.

Seedless Blackberry Jam

MAKES 3 HALF-PINTS

4½ cups fresh blackberries

2 cups sugar

Crush berries and heat until soft. Run the blackberries through a sieve or food mill and measure out 4 cups seedless pulp.

Combine pulp and sugar; cook rapidly, stirring constantly, until thick.

Ladle hot jam mixture quickly into the prepared jars, leaving ¼ inch headspace. Remove air bubbles by placing a nonmetallic spatula inside the jar and moving it from side to side and around the edge of the jar. Wipe jar rims and threads with a clean, damp paper towel; cover with two-piece lids, screwing bands tightly.

Process 15 minutes in a boiling-water canner; adjust for altitude if necessary.

SEEDLESS BLACKBERRY JAM

iStockphoto.com/kleiness

Spiced Grape Jam

MAKES 12 HALF-PINTS

SPICED GRAPE JAM
MSPhotographic/Fotolia

1 gallon grapes

9 cups sugar

1 tablespoon allspice

1 tablespoon cinnamon

1 tablespoon ground cloves

Run the grapes through a food mill to separate skins from pulp. Place the skins in one dish and the pulp in another. Cook the pulp without water until soft; run mixture through a food mill to remove seeds.

To the strained pulp, add the skins, sugar, allspice, cinnamon, and cloves. Boil together for 20 minutes.

Ladle hot jam mixture quickly into the prepared jars, leaving ¼ inch headspace. Remove air bubbles by placing a nonmetallic spatula inside the jar and moving it from side to side and around the edge of the jar. Wipe jar rims and threads with a clean, damp paper towel; cover with two-piece lids, screwing bands tightly.

Process 15 minutes in a boiling-water canner; adjust for altitude if necessary.

Easy Freezer Strawberry Jam

MAKES 4 HALF-PINTS

2 cups mashed strawberries

4 cups sugar or 3 cups sugar plus 1 cup honey

1 package fruit pectin

¾ cup water

Mix strawberries and sugar together thoroughly; let stand for 10 minutes.

Stir fruit pectin and water together in a saucepan; bring to a boil, stirring constantly, and boil for 1 minute. Remove from heat.

Stir strawberry mixture and pectin mixture together until sugar is completely dissolved and no longer grainy. Pour into plastic freezer containers and cover with tight lids. Let stand at room temperature before storing in the freezer.

Refrigerate after opening for up to 3 weeks.

Elderberry Jelly

MAKES 5 HALF-PINTS

6 quarts elderberries (about 3 pounds)

¼ cup lemon juice

4½ cups sugar

1 box (1¾ ounces) powdered pectin

½ teaspoon butter, optional

Discard stems and crush the berries. Place fruit in a saucepan. Heat over medium heat and slowly bring to a boil until juice starts to flow. Reduce heat; cover and simmer for 15 minutes, stirring occasionally.

Place a jelly bag or 3 layers of damp cheese-cloth in a large bowl. Pour in the cooked fruit. Hang the bag and let drain until dripping stops. Press gently to get all the juice squeezed out.

Measure 3 cups of elderberry juice into 6- or 8-quart saucepan. (Add up to ½ cup water to get the exact amount of juice needed if berries don't make enough juice.) Stir in lemon juice.

In separate bowl, measure sugar.

Stir pectin into juice in saucepan. Add butter to reduce foaming, if desired. Bring mixture to a full rolling boil over high heat, stirring constantly. Stir in sugar quickly. Return to full rolling boil and boil for exactly 1 minute, stirring constantly. Remove from heat. Skim off any foam with a metal spoon.

Ladle hot jelly mixture quickly into the prepared jars, leaving ¼ inch headspace. Remove air bubbles by placing a nonmetallic spatula inside the jar and moving it from side to side and around the edge of

ELDERBERRY JELLY

Lori Dunn

the jar. Wipe jar rims and threads with a clean, damp paper towel; cover with two-piece lids, screwing bands tightly.

Process for 5 minutes in boiling-water canner; adjust for altitude if necessary.

Low-Sugar Apple Cider Jelly

MAKES 5 HALF-PINTS

8 cups apple cider boiled down to 4 cups

1 cup apple cider

4 teaspoons calcium water (included in Pomona's Pectin box)

4 teaspoons Pomona's Pectin powder

Measure boiled-down apple cider into large saucepan. (Do not add 1 cup apple cider.)

Add calcium water to pan (see Pomona's directions for making calcium water) and stir well.

Bring 1 cup apple cider to a boil in a separate pan. Pour it into a blender or food processor and add the pectin powder. Vent the lid and blend 1 to 2 minutes until all powder is dissolved.

Bring boiled-down apple cider to a boil. Add pectin-cider mixture to pan and stir vigorously 1 to 2 minutes while cooking to dissolve pectin. Return to boil and remove from heat.

Ladle hot jelly mixture quickly into the prepared jars, leaving ¼ inch headspace. Remove air bubbles by placing a nonmetallic spatula inside the jar and moving it from side to side and around the edge of the jar. Wipe jar rims and threads with a clean, damp paper towel; cover with two-piece lids, screwing bands tightly.

Process 10 minutes in boiling-water canner; adjust for altitude if necessary.

Mint and Rhubarb Jelly

MAKES 7 TO 8 HALF-PINTS

3 pounds rhubarb, cut into 1-inch pieces

7½ cups sugar

1 cup packed spearmint leaves and stems

1 bottle fruit pectin

Put rhubarb in a large pan and cover with water. Cook until soft.

Place the rhubarb in a food processor and chop. Transfer rhubarb to a jelly cloth or bag suspended over a bowl. Squeeze out the juice and measure 3½ cups. Place juice and sugar in a large saucepan.

Put spearmint in a separate saucepan and press with a wooden potato masher or heavy glass, or crush lightly using a mortar and pestle. Add

spearmint to juice mixture. Heat over high heat to boiling.

As soon as mixture boils, add the pectin, stirring constantly. Bring to a full rolling boil and boil hard for 30 seconds. Remove from heat and skim foam.

Ladle hot jam mixture quickly into the prepared jars, leaving ¼ inch headspace. Remove air bubbles by placing a nonmetallic spatula inside the jar and moving it from side to side and around the edge of the jar. Wipe jar rims and threads with a clean, damp paper towel; cover with two-piece lids, screwing bands tightly.

Process 10 minutes in a boiling-water canner; adjust for altitude if necessary.

Mint Jelly

MAKES 4 HALF-PINTS

MINT JELLY

iStockphoto.com/Rainbohm

1½ cups firmly packed mint leaves with stems, washed

2¼ cups water

2 tablespoons fresh lemon juice

Few drops green food coloring, optional

3½ cups sugar

1 pouch liquid fruit pectin

Place mint leaves and stems in a 6- or 8-quart saucepan; crush leaves with a wooden spoon. Add the water and bring quickly to a boil. Remove from heat; cover and let stand for 10 minutes. Strain and measure 1¾ cups infusion into the saucepan. Add lemon juice, food coloring, and sugar; mix well.

Place pan over high heat and bring to a boil, stirring constantly. At once, stir in fruit pectin. Then bring to a full rolling boil and boil hard for 1 minute, stirring constantly. Remove from heat and skim off foam with a metal spoon.

Ladle hot jam mixture quickly into the prepared jars, leaving ¼ inch headspace. Remove air bubbles by placing a nonmetallic spatula inside the jar and moving it from side to side and around the edge of the jar. Wipe jar rims and threads with a clean, damp paper towel; cover with two-piece lids, screwing bands tightly.

Process 10 minutes in a boiling-water canner; adjust for altitude if necessary.

Pepper Jelly

MAKES 4 TO 5 HALF-PINTS

¼ cup ground hot peppers with seeds

¾ cup chopped green peppers

6½ cups sugar

1½ cups cider vinegar

1 bottle liquid pectin

Combine hot peppers, green peppers, sugar, and vinegar in a saucepan; boil for 3 minutes. Remove from heat and let stand for 5 minutes. Stir in pectin.

Ladle hot jam mixture quickly into the prepared jars, leaving ¼ inch headspace. Remove air bubbles by placing a nonmetallic spatula inside the jar and moving it from side to side and around the edge of the jar. Wipe jar rims and threads with a clean, damp paper towel; cover with two-piece lids, screwing bands tightly.

Process 10 minutes in boiling-water canner; adjust for altitude if necessary.

Spiced Blackberry Preserves

MAKES 5 TO 6 HALF-PINTS

SPICED BLACKBERRY PRESERVES
zigzagmtart/Fotolia

1 pound blackberries

2 cups sugar

1 tablespoon lemon juice

½ teaspoon cinnamon

⅛ teaspoon cloves

3 ounces liquid pectin
(½ of 6-ounce bottle)

Combine berries, sugar, lemon juice, and spices in a large saucepan. Bring to rolling boil and boil hard, uncovered, for 1 minute while stirring.

Remove pot from heat and stir in pectin. Skim foam.

Ladle hot preserve mixture quickly into the prepared jars, leaving ¼ inch headspace. Remove air bubbles by placing a nonmetallic spatula inside the jar and moving it from side to side and around the edge of the jar. Wipe jar rims and threads with a clean, damp paper towel; cover with two-piece lids, screwing bands tightly.

Process 15 minutes in a boiling-water canner; adjust for altitude if necessary.

Blackberries were free

I went to the Food Lion this summer and saw the blackberries: 4 dollars per pint. My mind traveled to the old days. I remember hearing that the old days were the good days. Now that I am 60, my young days are the good old days.

I had a wonderful grandmother and grandfather. They were energetic and resourceful. The land was less developed and the blackberry thickets covered the North Carolina Piedmont countryside.

It was always a special day when we picked blackberries. The day was always hot and dry. The white blossoms had long faded into plump blue, black, sweet berries. We covered our bodies completely to avoid the pricks and snake bites. Yes, the thickets were excellent habitat for snakes. I remember stepping on a few and fighting the fear. I never was bitten.

We all carried buckets. We didn't stop picking until our buckets were full. The bushes burst with berries so it really didn't consume an entire day. I couldn't resist eating the berries as I picked. So, I would have to say that my bucket was less full.

My grandmother had endless energy. Upon returning home, she immediately began to prepare the berries for cobbler and jam. I don't recall how she did it. I just remember the aftermath of jam on a hot biscuit with butter and the sweet cobbler with a glass of milk.

So, I see blackberries that are no longer free. But, my memories of the good old days are mine forever. I feel warm inside.

Kathy P. Sinning
Beaufort, North Carolina

Apricot Preserves

MAKES 4 HALF-PINTS

2 pounds apricots

1 pound crushed pineapple

3 pounds sugar

Scald, skin, and seed the apricots; place in a large saucepan. Add pineapple and sugar. Boil for 30 minutes, stirring occasionally to prevent sticking.

Ladle hot preserve mixture quickly into the prepared jars, leaving ¼ inch headspace. Remove air bubbles by placing a nonmetallic spatula inside the jar and moving it from side to side and around the edge of the jar. Wipe jar rims and threads with a clean, damp paper towel; cover with two-piece lids, screwing bands tightly.

APRICOT PRESERVES

Juststone JKaminska/Fotolia

Process 15 minutes in a boiling-water canner; adjust for altitude if necessary.

Old-Fashioned Tomato Preserves

MAKES 12 HALF-PINTS

5 pounds firm, ripe tomatoes

8 cups sugar

1 orange, sliced thin

1 lemon, sliced thin

Peel and quarter the tomatoes; cover with sugar and let stand overnight. Drain syrup into a saucepan and boil until it spins a thread, 232°F. Add the tomatoes, orange slices, and lemon slices. Cook over low heat until tomatoes are transparent, stirring frequently.

Ladle hot preserve mixture quickly into the prepared jars, leaving ¼ inch headspace. Remove air bubbles by placing a nonmetallic spatula inside the jar and moving it from side to side and around the edge of the jar. Wipe jar rims and threads with a clean, damp paper towel; cover with two-piece lids, screwing bands tightly.

Process 15 minutes in boiling-water canner; adjust for altitude if necessary.

Cranberry Chutney

MAKES 1 QUART

CRANBERRY CHUTNEY

Lori Dunn

1 pound fresh cranberries, rinsed

1 cup sugar

½ cup firmly packed light brown sugar

½ cup raisins

2 teaspoons ground cinnamon

1½ teaspoons ground ginger

½ teaspoon ground cloves

¼ teaspoon ground allspice

1 cup water

1 cup chopped sweet onion

1 cup chopped tart apple

½ cup chopped celery

In a large saucepan, combine cranberries, sugars, raisins, spices, and water; cook over medium heat until juice is released from cranberries, about 15 minutes. Stir frequently.

Add onions, apples, and celery; reduce heat to simmer. Cook, uncovered, for 15 minutes, until mixture thickens. Stir occasionally.

Refrigerate before serving.

Note: This chutney does not require processing. It will keep up to 2 weeks stored in an airtight container in the refrigerator.

Gooseberry Chutney Sauce

MAKES ABOUT 5 QUARTS

3 quarts gooseberries

2 cups seeded and chopped raisins

1 tablespoon salt

2 cups sugar

4 sweet green peppers, minced

¼ cup grated onion

3 cups vinegar

1 cup tart jelly

Juice of 4 lemons

1½ tablespoons ground ginger

½ teaspoon cayenne pepper

Crush the gooseberries slightly and place in a large saucepan. Add all remaining ingredients. Simmer until mixture is of the consistency of fruit butter.

Ladle hot chutney mixture quickly into the prepared jars, leaving ¼ inch headspace. Remove air bubbles by placing a nonmetallic spatula inside the jar and moving it from side to side and around the edge of the jar. Wipe jar rims and threads with a clean, damp paper towel; cover with two-piece lids, screwing bands tightly.

Process 10 minutes in boiling-water canner; adjust for altitude if necessary.

Slow Cooker Apple Butter

MAKES ABOUT 3 QUARTS

3 to 4 quarts peeled, cored, and finely chopped apples

4 cups sugar (or to taste)

4 teaspoons cinnamon

¼ teaspoon ground cloves

¼ teaspoon salt

Fill a slow cooker heaping full of apples. The lid may not fit in the beginning, but the apples shrink as they cook. Sprinkle sugar, cinnamon, cloves and salt over the apples.

Cover and cook on high for 1 hour; lower heat and continue cooking all day, or until the mixture is thick and dark in color, stirring occasionally. Fill small jars, leaving room for expansion. Cool and freeze.

SLOW COOKER APPLE BUTTER

iStockphoto.com/huePhotography

Pumpkin Butter

MAKES 10 HALF-PINTS

10 cups peeled pumpkin

Juice of 2 lemons

1 tablespoon
ground ginger

1 tablespoon
ground cinnamon

½ teaspoon
ground allspice

¾ teaspoon salt

2½ pounds
brown sugar

1 cup water

PUMPKIN BUTTER

iStockphoto.com/DebbiSmirnoff

Peel pumpkin and chop in a food processor. Transfer to a large saucepan. Add lemon juice, ginger, cinnamon, allspice, salt, and brown sugar. Cover and let stand overnight.

Add the water and boil gently until pumpkin is clear and mixture is thick.

Ladle hot butter mixture quickly into the prepared jars, leaving ¼ inch headspace. Remove air bubbles by placing a nonmetallic spatula inside the jar and moving it from side to side and around the edge of the jar. Wipe jar rims and threads with a clean, damp paper towel; cover with two-piece lids, screwing bands tightly.

Process 10 minutes in boiling-water canner; adjust for altitude if necessary.

Index